The Castle

The Castle

An Illustrated History
of the Smithsonian Building

Cynthia R. Field, Richard E. Stamm,

and Heather P. Ewing

Contributors

Linda NeCastro

Robert Esau

Phillip Kent

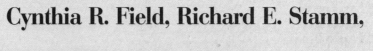

Smithsonian Institution Press
Washington and London

Designer: Janice Wheeler
Copy Editor: Susan M. S. Brown

Library of Congress Cataloging·in-
Publication Data
Field, Cynthia R.
    The Castle : an illustrated history of the
Smithsonian Building / Cynthia R. Field,
Richard E. Stamm, and Heather P. Ewing.
        p.   cm.
    Includes bibliographical references and
index.
    ISBN 1-56098-287-X (pbk. : alk. paper)
    1. Smithsonian Institution Building (Wash-
ington, D.C.) 2. Public buildings—Washington (D.C.) 3. Washington (D.C.)—Buildings,
structures, etc. I. Stamm, Richard E. II. Ewing, Heather P. III. Title.
NA4227.W2F53   1993
727'.6'0009753—dc20   92-45811

British Library Cataloguing-in-Publication
Data is available

Manufactured in the United States of
America
00 99 98 97 96 95 94 93   5 4 3 2 1

⊗ The paper used in this publication meets
the minimum requirements of the American
National Standard for Permanence of Paper
for Printed Library Materials Z39.48-1984

The cover, title spread, and various section
opening pages include images or details of images that duplicate figures described and
credited elsewhere in the text. For complete
caption and credit information, see the following: cover, see Fig. 26 (p. 19); pp. ii–iii, see
Fig. 67 (p. 56); p. xviii, see Fig. 164 (p. 144);
pp. 2–3, see Fig. 16 (p. 10); pp. 22–23, see
Fig. 33 (p. 27); pp. 52–53, see Fig. 68 (p. 56);
pp. 94–95, see Fig. 113 (p. 99); pp. 120–21,
see Fig. 153 (p. 134).

Contents

To the Contributing Members and all those who share our interest in this distinguished building and in the Smithsonian Institution, of which it is the symbol

Acknowledgments

The Office of Architectural History and Historic Preservation is grateful to the many individuals who have supported this work. The authors particularly wish to thank the following, without whom this book would not have been possible: Richard L. Siegle, Director of Facilities Services, for his support; Nancy Suttenfield, Assistant Secretary for Finance and Administration, for her interest; Jim Hobbins, who suggested the project and, along with Susan Bradley, reviewed the manuscript; Joe Carper and Fern Segerlind of Contributing Membership for their encouragement.

Our office colleagues Amy Ballard, Michael Hendron, and Peter Muldoon provided assistance in ways too numerous to list. Our former graduate interns Robert Esau, Phillip Kent, and Linda NeCastro contributed their research projects for us to use in the text as we saw fit. We thank them for their generosity. Special thanks to Stuart Furman of Facilities Services for his meticulous proofreading.

The staff of the Office of Printing and Photographic Services deserves our special thanks, especially Richard Strauss for his beautiful photographs of selected rooms, along with Dane Penland, Jeff Tinsley, Rick Vargas, and a host of interns. The printing of each negative required the skills of John Dillaber, Richard Smart, John Steiner, Edes Hugh Talman, and Louie Thomas. David Burgevin of the photographic library proved especially helpful in locating hard-to-find negatives, and Mary Ellen McCaffrey was the glue that held this operation together.

The staff of the Smithsonian Institution Archives assisted us in a variety of research tasks. We thank all the members of this office—especially Bill Cox, Bill Deiss, Libby Glenn, Pam Henson, Josephine Jameson, Shawn Johnstone, Bruce Kirby, James Steed, Diane Vogt-O'Connor, and Ashley Wyant—for handling our endless inquiries with patience and understanding.

Other research centers of the Institution were extremely important to this work. Kathleen Dorman, Marc Rothenberg, John Rumm, and Paul Theerman of the Joseph Henry Papers were generous with their expertise throughout the project. The Smithsonian Libraries were called upon to order an extraordinary number of books, which they did with the greatest efficiency.

Other Smithsonian colleagues assisted us over the months of writing. Tom Crouch and David DeVorkin shared their enthusiasm about and knowledge of the Smithsonian's early astrophysical projects. Our special thanks to Paula Fleming for generously sharing her research. With her knowledge of stereo views, Susan Myers made particularly crucial contributions. We are grateful to Ildiko DeAngelis, Margaret Gaynor, Patricia Graboske, Francis Greenwell, Dan Nicolson, Craig Orr, Vic Springer, and Helena Wright, who shared their work with us. Thanks to Dr. William Sturtevant for his keen eyesight and insight into the museum exhibitions of the late nineteenth century, as well as to others in the Anthropology Department, especially Molly Coxson, Chang-Su Houchins, and Jane Walsh. Our gratitude to Ellis Yochelson for leading us to Susan Glassman, and to her for graciously supplying us with information on the lecture hall of the Wagner-Free Institute. Thanks also to Betty Youssef and Ted Rivinus for sharing *Spencer Baird of the Smithsonian* while it was still in manuscript.

During our research we called upon a variety of institutions and people for their assistance. We would like to thank as many as we can, and ask forgiveness for any inadvertent omissions. The Architect of the Capitol, Records Office; Ronald Borjeson, Worcester Historical Museum Library; R. Jeanne Cobb, archivist, and Dana Garner, photographer, Bethany College, West Virginia; Raymond Cotton, National Archives; Patrice Donahue, curatorial associate, Harvard University Archives; Teresa Grana; Richard H. Howland; Cliff Krainik; John J. McDonough, who led us to the diary of young Francis Ormand French; Caryl Marsh; Nina D. Myatt, curator of Antioch College; Ariel Brun de Pontet; Susan Sutton, Indiana Historical Society; Pam Wasmer, Indiana Division, Indiana State Library; and Linda Ziemer, Chicago Historical Society. Our valued colleagues Pamela Scott and James Goode have consistently contributed their suggestions throughout the project.

For unfailing assistance and technical wizardry, we offer heartfelt thanks to Asher Gendelman and Mike Schultz.

We are grateful to the distinguished architectural historian William H. Pierson, Jr., for being our model of scholarly method and for unfailing generosity of spirit in sharing with us his own formidable research. We are honored that he has contributed the introduction to this book.

For sustenance, transportation, and general interest, we are grateful to Charles G. Field.

Thanks finally to Susan M. S. Brown, Duke Johns, Amy Pastan, and Janice Wheeler, who saw us along the way from start to finish.

Chronology

The act of Congress that authorized the Smithsonian Institution, dated August 10, 1846, was a legislative compromise devised to fulfill multiple functions. The Smithsonian Building, which we have come to know as "the Castle," was originally designed to house a library, a museum, a gallery of art, and a lecture hall, and to realize the multiple expectations of the founders. With each era of growth and change, the building's appearance was altered along with its role. At first the Smithsonian was a research institution with a museum, but soon the expanding museum collections outgrew the building, necessitating new construction. With each new museum building, the role of the original Smithsonian Building was reconsidered. In its second century, the Smithsonian Building has been transformed into the administrative heart and the symbol of a multifaceted institution.

From the details of the 1846 legislation, the Smithsonian Institution emerged with the imprimatur of the United States and certain national responsibilities but no overt affiliation with the federal government. The laying of the cornerstone, using the Masonic ceremonial regalia that had belonged to George Washington, in the presence of President Polk and members of his Cabinet, emphasized the Smithsonian's place in the executive family. The enabling legislation and the composition of the Board of Regents that it mandated, however, signaled that the Smithsonian was an independent establishment.

The legislation directed the Board to elect a Secretary of the Institution, who inherited the problems created by this joint federal and private identity. The Secretary immediately became the single most influential force on the direction of the Smithsonian. The Institution's historical development can be divided into eras shaped by the interests of its Secretaries, whose impact has also been reflected in the architectural evolution of the Smithsonian's original building.

1829
James Smithson died in Genoa, Italy, on June 27.

1835
The United States was notified of the Smithson bequest.

1838
The bequest, over half a million dollars, was brought to the United States. Congress began debate on how to realize Smithson's intent.

1845
Robert Dale Owen and David Dale Owen collaborated on a plan for a Smithsonian building.

1846
Congress passed the act organizing the Smithsonian Institution. The Building Committee of the Board of Regents selected the plans of James Renwick, Jr. The Regents invited Professor Joseph Henry, of Princeton University, to be Secretary of the Smithsonian.

1. Portrait of Joseph Henry, Secretary from 1846 to 1878, photograph. Smithsonian Institution Archives, neg. SA-16.

2. Portrait of Spencer Fullerton Baird, Secretary from 1878 to 1887, photograph. Smithsonian Institution Archives, neg. SA-243.

3. Portrait of Samuel Pierpont Langley, Secretary from 1887 to 1906, photograph. Smithsonian Institution, neg. 10616.

Joseph Henry, the first Secretary (1846–78), found the resources devoted to the Smithsonian Building a drain on his effort to establish a great research institution. He contained the costs of the building by reducing its height and altering extensively its interior design. Henry also attempted to maintain a physical separation between the Institution's public functions and its scientific research endeavors. After the transfer of government collections resulted in the establishment of the National Museum in the Smithsonian Building, Henry sought to preserve separate identities for the museum and the Smithsonian. He established this division first within the Smithsonian Building and subsequently by moving the public functions of library, gallery of art, and lecture hall out of the building altogether.

Even before becoming Secretary, Spencer Fullerton Baird (1878–87), who had been at the Smithsonian since 1850, encouraged and then supervised the creation of a new building solely devoted to the National Museum (now the Arts and Industries Building), which relieved the overcrowded original Smithsonian Building. In his nine years at the helm, Baird, as recent biographers have averred, emphasized the museum side of the Institution. He directed resources into expanding the collections and supporting collections-related research while sharply decreasing funds for other independent scientific research.[1] The Smithsonian Building continued to be devoted primarily to collections, which were rearranged to accommodate more space for curatorial research.

Secretary Samuel Pierpont Langley (1887–1906) revived the Smithsonian's charter to house an art gallery with the installation in the building of the Art Room and the aborted effort to create a national gallery of art in the Upper Main Hall. Langley's interest in reaching new audiences resulted in the creation of a children's museum in the Smithsonian Building, as well as the National Zoological Park (now located in Rock Creek Park), which began in the building's backyard.

4. Portrait of Charles Doolittle Walcott, Secretary from 1907 to 1927, photograph. Smithsonian Institution, neg. 83-14114.

Two new buildings, the Freer Gallery of Art and a second national museum building (which later came to be called the National Museum of Natural History), were completed during the years Charles Doolittle Walcott was Secretary (1907–27). The transfer of natural history collections into the new building once again caused a reallocation of functions in the original Smithsonian Building.

1847
The cornerstone of the building was laid on May 1. The exterior of the East Wing and Range was completed by December 31.

1848
The West Wing and Range were under construction in August. Also in August the foundation of the Main Building was begun.

1849
The East Wing and Range were completed and occupied.

1850
The West Wing and Range were completed and occupied. The Main Building was roofed and the towers partially completed. Part of the Lower Main Hall collapsed during construction. An investigation recommended that the building be completed with fireproof materials.

1851
The exterior of the building was completed.

1852
The Regents determined that Renwick's compensation had been authorized through 1852 only and declined to renew his contract. Barton S. Alexander of the Corps of Engineers took over the fireproof construction of the building.

1855
With the opening of the Lower Main Hall to the public, the entire building was completed and occupied. The Henry apartments were constructed in the East Wing.

1857
The first guidebook to the Smithsonian, illustrating many of the building's interior spaces, was published.

1858
The cloisters on the north facade were enclosed. The galleries and cases in the Lower Main Hall were completed and arranged to house the National Museum after the transfer of the collections of the National Institute.

1865
A massive fire on January 24 destroyed the Upper Main Hall and primary towers with their contents. Adolf Cluss was appointed architect for the renovation. Over the next two years, he reconstructed the South Tower, inserting three floors to double the office space and adding iron columns for support. He also reinforced the North Towers with a brick lining, inserted an additional floor above the entrance, and designed an elaborate cast-iron stairway for the North Hall.

5. Portrait of Charles Greeley Abbot, Secretary from 1928 to 1944, photograph. Smithsonian Institution, neg. 42563.

1867

The iron and slate roof designed by Cluss for the Main Building was completed. With the exception of the Upper Main Hall, the reconstruction of the building was finished.

1871

The floor of the West Wing was reconstructed with fireproof materials and raised to provide basement laboratories for Natural History.

1872

Reconstruction of the Upper Main Hall was completed. The East Wing and Range were cleared of all museum-related functions.

1874

Paintings, statuary, and engravings belonging to the Institution were deposited with the Corcoran Gallery of Art.

1878

Joseph Henry died and Spencer Fullerton Baird was appointed Secretary.

1881

The National Museum Building was completed and opened to the public. Overcrowding in the Smithsonian Building was relieved by the transfer of specimens to the new building.

1882

The galleries of the Lower Main Hall were changed from exhibition to curators' space.

1884

In the course of fireproofing, the East Wing and Range were reconfigured and enlarged by Adolf Cluss and Paul Schulze.

1887

The West Range was fireproofed by Cluss & Schulze. Samuel Pierpont Langley was appointed Secretary.

1891

The West Wing roof was rebuilt with fireproof materials.

1901

The Children's Room was opened on the first floor of the South Tower.

1903

The Art Room on the second floor of the East Wing was completed.

1905

The Crypt containing Smithson's remains was created at the north entrance.

1907

Charles Doolittle Walcott was appointed Secretary. A proposal was made to house a national gallery of art in the Upper Main Hall and a sculpture hall in the West Wing.

During the Depression and the war years, Secretary Charles Greeley Abbot (1928–44) maintained the buildings and programs of the Smithsonian. He expanded the building's capacity by housing the new Division of Radiation and Organisms, which resulted from his own research interests, in the basement and highest tower. In 1940 Abbot first used public space in the Smithsonian Building for information services by creating the "Index Exhibit" to guide visitors through the complexities of the Institution.

6. Portrait of Alexander Wetmore, Secretary from 1945 to 1952, photograph. Smithsonian Institution, neg. 82-3138.

7. Portrait of Leonard Carmichael, Secretary from 1953 to 1964, photograph. Smithsonian Institution, neg. 82-1134.

Smithsonian endeavors in the postwar years under Secretary Alexander Wetmore (1945–52) did not lead in the direction of physical expansion. Having become Assistant Secretary of the Smithsonian in 1925, Wetmore as Secretary devoted many years to the administrative aspects of managing the growth of the collections, the increase of visitors, and the limitations of funding. His vision was not within the Smithsonian Building but fixed on a research center for Smithsonian scientists and curators, which would be located away from the National Mall.

Secretary Leonard Carmichael's (1953–64) aggressive exhibition modernization campaign was showcased in another new museum building, the Museum of History and Technology (now the National Museum of American History), resulting in a threefold growth in the annual number of visitors to the Smithsonian. Modernization of the original Smithsonian Building was initiated at this time to improve the aging physical plant and make public areas more attractive to the Institution's increased audience.

In his annual report for 1959, the Secretary stated:

More and more museums are seen as places needed to inspire each new generation with the kind of patriotisr: that is based on a valid understanding of the factors that have led to national growth. . . . This new museum philosophy has been wholeheartedly accepted and adopted at the Smithsonian.[2]

1911
Transfer of natural history specimens from the Smithsonian Building was made possible by the completion of a new National Museum Building (later the National Museum of Natural History).

1914
Renovation of the Lower Main Hall included new lighting and removal of the galleries.

1915
The exterior of the building was repointed and windows were repaired.

1916
The Lower Main Hall was reopened with Graphic Arts exhibits, and the library was established on new steel book stacks at either end of the hall.

1928
Charles Greeley Abbot was appointed Secretary.

1940
The Lower Main Hall was renovated and completely redecorated for the "Index Exhibit." Thirty feet at each end of the hall were enclosed to conceal steel book stacks and office space.

1945
Alexander Wetmore was appointed Secretary.

8. Portrait of S. Dillon Ripley, Secretary from 1964 to 1984, photograph. Smithsonian Institution, neg. 57272.

9. Portrait of Robert McCormick Adams, Secretary from 1984 to the present, photograph. Smithsonian Institution, neg. 89-5855-2.

Secretary S. Dillon Ripley (1964–84) returned a portion of the Smithsonian Building to Joseph Henry's vision of a setting for scholars with a proposed Center for Advanced Study in the renovated Upper Main Hall. Following the tradition set by his twentieth-century predecessors, Ripley expanded and enhanced the building's facilities to assist the ever-increasing number of Smithsonian visitors. He also restored the public and administrative spaces with appropriate Victorian finishes and furnishings. He used the building, affectionately known by then as the Castle, as a symbol of the Smithsonian Institution itself.

Robert McCormick Adams, who became Secretary in 1984, extended the focus of attention beyond the confines of the Castle. When he approved placing an expanded and centralized information center in the Great Hall, the Smithsonian Building was transformed into the public and administrative hub of the Institution.

1953

Leonard Carmichael was appointed Secretary.

1956

The windows in the Lower Main Hall were replaced.

1963

At the request of the Smithsonian, the General Services Administration prepared a feasibility study for the renovation of the Smithsonian Building.

1964

All remaining public museum exhibits in the Smithsonian Building were transferred to the newly constucted National Museum of History and Technology. S. Dillon Ripley was appointed Secretary.

1965

The Department of Botany was moved from the Upper Main Hall to the newly completed wing on the Natural History Building. Chatelain, Gauger & Nolan were selected as architects for the renovation.

1970

Renovation of the building was completed. The roof on the lower North Tower was restored using old photographs. The Woodrow Wilson International Center for Scholars was installed in newly created floors occupying the former Upper Main Hall.

1971

The West Wing was opened as the Commons, a dining facility for staff and Contributing Members.

1980

A nineteenth-century statue of St. Dunstan, restored after arrival from Westminster Abbey, was installed in the niche on the South Tower.

1984

Robert McCormick Adams was appointed Secretary.

1987

The Great Hall was renovated and opened as the Visitor Information and Associates' Reception Center.

1988

A restoration of the Children's Room was completed.

1992

Repointing of the exterior and the window renovation project were completed.

Introduction

By 1845 the architecture of Washington, D.C., was dominated by the vigorous presence of Robert Mills, whose Treasury, Patent Office, and General Post Office buildings all carried forward the classical principles that had marked official Washington from the time of its inception in the late eighteenth century. In spite of its raw edges, the slowly emerging city had developed the first signs of a coherent architectural order. It was light in tone, with authentic classical details cut crisply into the warm Aquia stone that was used for most early government buildings. Against this, at midcentury, the dark red sandstone towers and battlements of the Romanesque Smithsonian Building appeared with stunning impact, interrupting the line of classical descent and promising instead a wholly new direction for American architecture. This dramatic shift in architectural values represented the arrival of the doctrine of the picturesque in the architecture of a classicistic institutional setting.

The client for the Smithsonian was a scientific/cultural institution held in trust for the American people by the government. The Smithsonian Institution was made possible by a remarkable bequest from a British experimental scientist, James Smithson. When he died in 1829, his entire estate was left to a nephew with the provision that should his heir die without issue the property would then be bequeathed "to the United States of America, to found at Washington, under the name of the Smithsonian Institution, an Establishment for the increase and diffusion of knowledge among men." The nephew died a bachelor in 1835. After considerable debate in Congress, and several years of litigation in the English Court of Chancery, the money was turned over to Richard Rush, special agent of the U.S. government appointed to receive these funds. With accrued interest, the amount was reported at the time to be $515,169. As soon as the Smithsonian bequest arrived in the United States in 1838, a controversy erupted in Congress about what the benefactor had in mind.

The major disagreement was over the intent of the will as expressed in the critical phrase "to found . . . an Establishment for the increase and diffusion of knowledge among men." John Quincy Adams fought valiantly for the establishment of an astronomical observatory. Senator Rufus Choate stood just as firmly for the creation of a great national library. Senator Benjamin Tappan drafted a bill to use the fund for an educational institution dedicated to the practical sciences, agriculture chief among them. Congressman Robert Dale Owen hoped for an institution to train teachers for a nationwide system of free secondary schools.[1] Throughout the debate, the creation of a building remained a given while the programs it would house were weighed.

The story of the building itself, therefore, is one of democracy at work in the realm of public architecture. At its best, it is one of conflicting ideas and ideals of dedicated, well-meaning public servants striving to reconcile differences that were sometimes irreconcilable; at its worst, it is the story of those same men struggling, accusing, even scheming to outmaneuver one another in order to have things right the way each saw it. In the end, it is the story of the history of a building, as it was modified and changed, damaged and rebuilt in response to the ravages of fate and the shifting direction of those in control. The miracle is that it survived at all, but survive it did, to stand as a seminal landmark in American public architecture.

William H. Pierson, Jr.

1. Evolution of the Design

*G*iving physical form to the broad mandate for "the increase and diffusion of knowledge among men" presented the governing board of the Smithsonian with a formidable task. The numerous functions imposed by Congress after lengthy debate required a building unlike any in midnineteenth-century America. Eager to put forth his own vision for the Smithsonian Building, Regent Robert Dale Owen transformed the vague directions into a specific program. His brother, David Dale Owen, helped him translate the program into a proto-plan, which laid out a series of spaces to accommodate the needs of a museum, a gallery of art, a library, and a teaching and research facility. Commensurate in importance with this effort was the expression of the plan in a medieval revival architectural form.

This conceptual design, annotated by the architect of public buildings Robert Mills, was presented for development to numerous architects in the United States. Of the designs submitted that of James Renwick, Jr., most sensitively responded to all the requirements.

During a period in American architecture when a building's style was meant to evoke an underlying message, the choice of a medieval revival style was a deliberate identification with collegiate typology. This decision was confirmed repeatedly through the evolution of the design. In contrast to classical public buildings, which evoked ancient democracies, the Smithsonian took on a form related to the late medieval English university, denoting the combination of private funds with public function.

*P*rogrammatic ideas for a Smithsonian building began to take shape years before the establishment in 1846 of the Institution: museum, gallery of art, astronomical observatory, national library, agricultural college, teacher training institution. Each of these programs would have necessitated a distinctive space: a tall and unobstructed room for the museum, skylighted art galleries, a domed space for the observatory, a well-lit, lofty space for the library, and lecture halls for teaching courses suitable to an agriculture college or teacher training institution.

Over an eight-year period, from 1838 through 1845, eleven bills were tabled before Congress finally acted to give practical form to James Smithson's bequest. During that time, two preliminary designs for a Smithsonian building were put forward, one by Robert Mills, architect of numerous public buildings, and one by Robert Dale Owen and his brother, David Dale Owen, who was one of the nation's leading field geologists. The two plans represented the development of a physical reality for the concept of a Smithsonian Institution.

■

As early as 1841, Robert Mills submitted a plan for a building to house a Smithsonian Institution, which would be integrated with the National Institute for the Promotion of Science. The National Institute, created by an act of Congress in 1841, was a private organization for the collection of natural history specimens that required ample exhibition space along with lecture halls and an observatory. In his *Discourse on the Objects and Importance of the National Institution for the Promotion of Science,* its president, Joel Poinsett, explained:

The lovers of science, literature, and the fine arts, residing in the District, felt sensibly the absence of those resources which are found elsewhere, and are necessary for the attainment of knowledge. They . . . formed an association, and applied themselves to collect specimens of geology and mineralogy, and other objects of natural history. . . . The Insti-

10. Robert Mills, National Institute with Smithsonian Institution Building, rendering, February 1841. National Archives, Record Group 77, neg. 90-4.

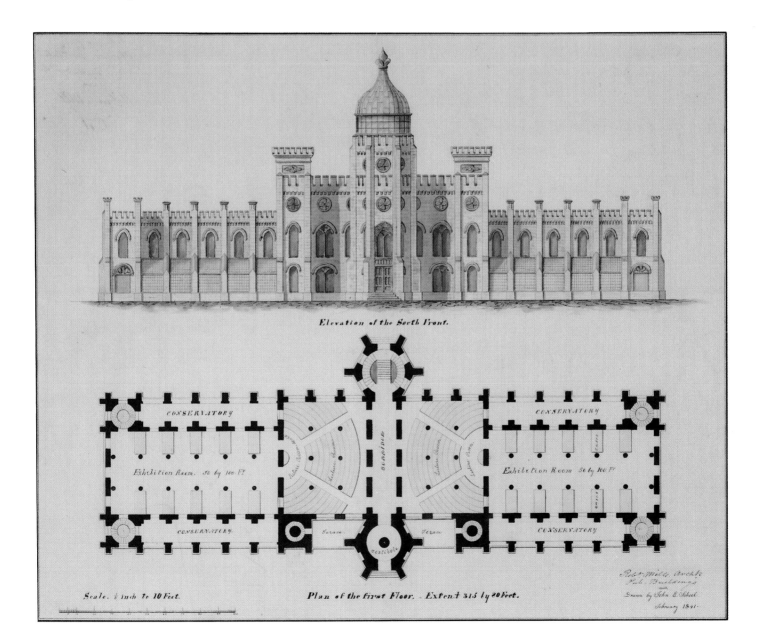

Elevation of the South Front.

Scale. ½ inch to 10 Feet.   *Plan of the first Floor. — Extent 315 by 90 Feet.*

11. Portrait of Robert Dale Owen, photograph, date unknown. Indiana Historical Society.

12. Portrait of David Dale Owen, drawing, 1852. Picture Collection, Indiana State Library.

tution for the Promotion of Science and the Useful Arts, will, as its name indicates, embrace every branch of knowledge.[1]

Rather than the classical style of the numerous public buildings he had designed for the U.S. government, Mills used a romantic medieval style to establish the distinction between the Institution and the government buildings. He based his Smithsonian proposal on his 1839 plan for a library and observatory at West Point. The most arresting feature of the West Point building was the double curve or ogee dome housing the observatory, which Mills modeled on Tom Tower of Christ Church (College) at Oxford University.[2] The association of this feature with a university was surely intended, because Mills envisioned the building as part of a complex for an agricultural college.[3] By placing all the stairs in the towers, he created a large, uninterrupted museum space on the top floor to house the National Institute's collections. The choice of a medieval revival style and the effective use of towers for circulation remained central to the later design development of the Smithsonian Building.

■

Because he was especially concerned that the Smithsonian Building be a fit expression of its functions, Robert Dale Owen was in correspondence with his brother, David Dale Owen, as early as August 1845 to develop a preliminary plan. Intending the Institution to function as a

center for free public education and to include a training center for teachers, Robert Dale Owen identified features that would remain in the planning process: four or five lecture rooms, including one for chemistry with a student laboratory and another for geology with provision for using large-scale visual aids, and a meeting room for the governing board. This all-encompassing plan included also sizable spaces for a museum, a library, conservatories, and an astronomical observatory. A medieval college was conjured up through Owen's evocative request for a "piazza, or cloister, for the use of students in wet weather . . . in keeping with the style of architecture suggested."[4]

Robert Dale Owen proposed they adopt from Robert Mills's plan the uninterrupted museum room that ran the length of the building's central block. He also adopted Mills's suggestion for an "Anglo-

Saxon" style, redefining the term by saying, "I believe, that, by going back to the pure Norman, with its Saxon arches & simple forms, you may provide something well suited for the purposes in view."[5]

■

While David Dale Owen's plans have been lost, the detailed description he wrote to accompany his design of October 10, 1845, remains. His building consisted of a central block three stories high with wings on each side connected to the main body by low stretches called "ranges."[6] On the third floor were two mixed-use rooms for demonstration lectures, specimen exhibitions, and the gallery of art; on the second floor was a large museum space for the natural history objects; on the first story were the library stacks area, a reading room, and a lecture hall seating 700 to 800 people.

of the Smithsonian Institution agreeably to the Design

13. Robert Mills, "(Perspective of) the Smithsonian Institution, agreeably to the design . . . ," rendering, 1846. Smithsonian Institution Archives, color transparency in the Collection of the Office of Architectural History and Historic Preservation.

At Robert Dale Owen's request, Robert Mills completed another design for the Smithsonian in September 1846, after having reviewed David Dale Owen's plans and drawings. In his revised design, Mills adopted the wings and ranges of Owen's layout. The medieval revival style and the staircase towers were retained. Battlements and buttresses suggested the early English medieval, while the mix of window treatments—round-headed, pointed, square-headed—spanned four centuries. Mills acknowledged that "our associations with great literary institutions are assimilated with the Saxon style of architecture in these buildings."[7]

With the exception of locating a lecture hall in the central block, Mills arranged the space as Owen had: a library on the first floor, a museum on the second, and galleries for art and demonstration lecture rooms on the third. Mills planned to accommodate four lecture halls, along with attached offices, in the wings. The "piazzas" remained on the north side and, unseen in this drawing, the conservatories on the south. Mills introduced a niche over the entrance for a statue of James Smithson. The observatory, which had occasioned the distinctive dome of the 1841 proposal, was now situated in the octagonal stair tower on the north side, which was also to have a great clock.

Under Robert Dale Owen's leadership, the Smithsonian's Board of Regents, on which Owen served as head of the Building Committee, rapidly selected both site and building. On September 9, 1846, only two days after the Board's first meeting, Owen presented his brother's plan, with drawings and specifications, as well as Mills's refinement. News of the proposed architectural commission was published in Washington newspapers, although word of the project had already spread among architects and builders.[8]

To obtain plans for a Smithsonian Building from a wide range of established architects as quickly as possible, Robert Dale Owen and other members of the Building Committee embarked on a tour of the northeastern states. The Owen drawings were shown along with descriptive specifications in the form of the Owen brothers' edited correspondence. From the evidence of some of the competition drawings, it seems likely that the Mills scheme of 1846 was also shown. Certain elements—such as the carriage porch, skylights for the lecture halls, an exhibition space for Smithson memorabilia, and an office for the Secretary—appeared in neither design but were mentioned in these discussions. A special plea was made to have the whole structure designed to be reasonably fireproof.[9] Among the architects visited on this trip was twenty-eight-year-old James Renwick, Jr., highly regarded for his Gothic Grace Church in New York City.

14. James Renwick, Jr., Smithsonian Building, North Elevation in the Gothic style and Plan, drawing, 1846. Smithsonian Institution Archives, Smithsonian Institution, neg. 92-9495.

Already sympathetic with the organization of spaces and the decidedly romantic articulation of the facades, Renwick might have executed this, his earliest scheme, as a building in the Gothic style, even before the Building Committee's September trip. Several elements suggest the influence of Robert Mills's 1841 design.[10] Like the Mills plan, Renwick's sketch featured a tower modeled on the Oxford example of Christ Church and depicted a building only two stories high, although the Owen plan called for three stories. Had he already met with the Building Committee, Renwick would have understood that they preferred a clearly Romanesque style over the early Gothic style favored by Mills. As might be expected of someone who had not yet learned of the Owens' program for the building, Renwick set forth largely undifferentiated spaces, with the exception of two lecture halls to the south of each wing.

**15. James Renwick, Jr.,
Auditorium for Smithsonian
Building, drawing, 1846.**
Smithsonian Institution Archives,
Smithsonian Institution, neg. 92-9492.

The lecture halls had been important to the development of the Owen brothers' plan, representing a means of providing free public education to all. With this sketch, Renwick appeared to have been working out aspects of the Mills-Owen plan discussed on the Building Committee's trip. The amphitheater configuration of the lecture hall existed in Mills's 1841 project. David Dale Owen's specifications also included a semicircular theater for lectures in anatomy on the third story of his central building. Whatever source he used, Renwick was now paying close attention to the requirements of the competition models.

16. James Renwick, Jr., Smithsonian Building, South Elevation in the Romanesque style, drawing, 1846. Smithsonian Institution Archives, Smithsonian Institution, neg. 92-9500.

Renwick's winning entry was likely quite close to this drawing.[11] The Romanesque scheme provided three stories, to accommodate the library on the first floor, the museum on the second, and the gallery of art on the third floor. Renwick's use of buttresses, which deflect the thrust of interior masonry vaults, suggested that he had employed vaulting to provide the fireproof construction requested by the Building Committee on their visit. The south tower in the center of the building featured a protruding bay known as an oriel window for the Regents' Room in the shape selected by Robert Dale Owen from the antiquarian John Henry Parker's *A Glossary of Terms used in Grecian, Roman, Italian and Gothic Architecture.*[12] Renwick's placement of the open cloistered walkways or "piazzas" on the south side rather than on the north as in the Owen-Mills plan may have stemmed from an effort to avoid the shadier side of the building.

17. James Renwick, Jr., East Elevation, drawing, 1846.

Smithsonian Institution Archives, Smithsonian Institution, neg. 92-9483.

Robert Dale Owen considered the east end an example of the whole design approach he advocated, letting the style of the architecture be adapted to the plan to enhance the building's fitness to function:[13]

The entire rectangle of that wing was laid out as a Chemical Lecture-room, with a gallery on three sides. . . . It was decided, that the seats in the main body of the Lecture-room should be placed on an inclined surface, rising to the gallery floor and connecting with it; and that the usual entrance for the audience should be, not below, where delicate and fragile apparatus was exposed, but by a staircase to the gallery floor, whence the audience should descend, on either side of the inclined plane, to its seats. To carry into effect this arrangement, a stairway outside the Lecture-room was required. It was obtained within a porch projecting from the eastern front; and as, in a porch of suitable proportions, the requisite height could not be gained without making the stairs too steep, a small outer porch was added, with a few steps therein.

Thus the peculiarities of internal adaptation in this wing stamped upon its eastern elevation the exterior it now presents; the general effect being, I think, pleasing and harmonious.[14]

The chimneys in this drawing contained flues for the smelting operations that were to be part of the chemical laboratories located in this area. Renwick's design for

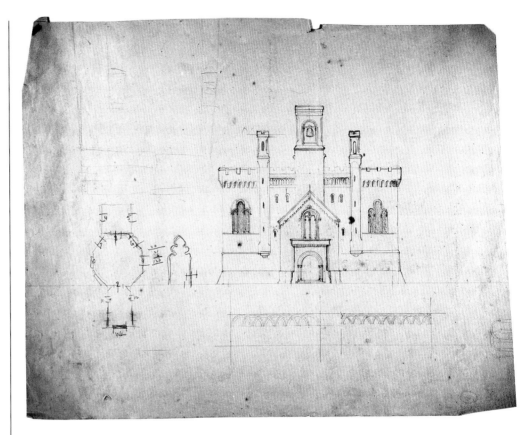

the chimneys mimicked the form of the bell tower in the center, which was described as "Norman."[15] In addition, Renwick described the interlaced arches between the chimneys as "Norman" in his specifications to the stonecutters.[16]

Although the architects had been told to submit their plans to the Board of Regents by December 25, the Building Committee had already settled on Renwick's design by November 30.[17] This premature selection caused what Henry called "a tempest among the architects,"[18] but the reason for Renwick's victory was clear. Designs that failed to adhere to the

Owen-Mills "Norman" model were all losers; only Renwick's design included, as the Building Committee explained, "all the accommodations demanded by the charter."[19]

18. James Renwick, Jr., Model for Smithsonian Building from the north, 1846. Collection of the Office of Architectural History and Historic Preservation, Smithsonian Institution, neg. x3915.

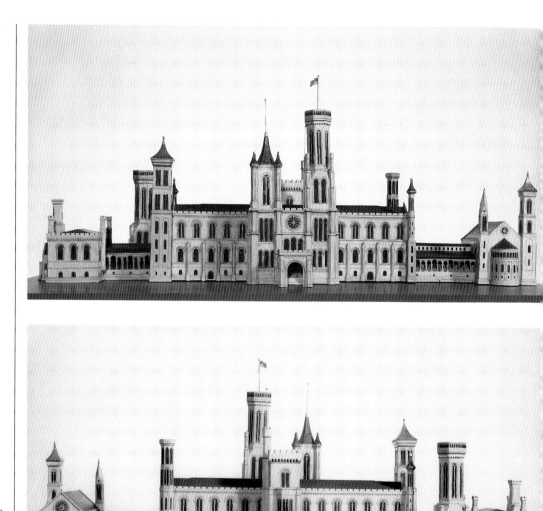

19. James Renwick, Jr., Model for Smithsonian Building from the south, 1846. Collection of the Office of Architectural History and Historic Preservation, Smithsonian Institution, neg. x3917.

Cost became a dominant design factor with the selection of Joseph Henry, a distinguished professor of physics at Princeton University, as the Smithsonian's Secretary.[20] Henry's interpretation of "increase and diffusion of knowledge among men" differed radically from that of Robert Dale Owen. Henry believed that "increase" meant the "discovery of new truths" by original research and that "diffusion" would properly be handled through scholarly publication. Soon he concluded that the building would drain the slender resources he believed should be dedicated to the creation of the Institution itself.

Upon his arrival in December 1846 to take up the position of Secretary, Henry attempted to halt the building plans. His goal was to prevent the deflection of Smithsonian funds from research into the building.[21] As a result of his efforts to convince the Board to erect a much less costly building, the plans were altered to cut the central building from three stories to two.[22]

Renwick's model, submitted with his entry in 1846, presented the scheme that the Building Committee had selected.[23] By the time the presentation renderings

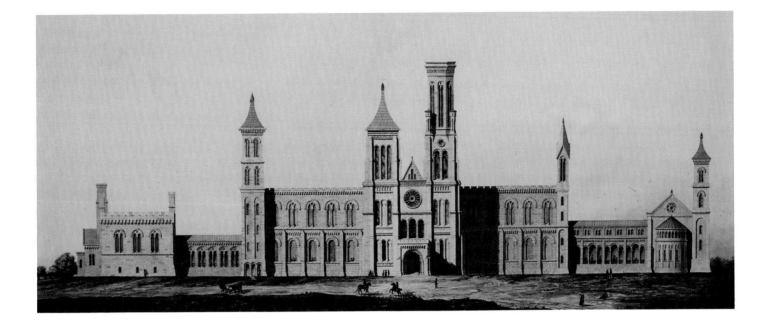

**20. James Renwick, Jr.,
Smithsonian Building, North
Facade, rendering, painted by
Louis Townsend and drawn by
H. C. Moore, June 1848.** Smithsonian
Institution Archives, color slide in the
Collection of the Office of Architectural
History and Historic Preservation.

were made in 1848, Renwick had reduced
the building to two stories by removing
the windowed ground-level floor. Also
eliminated were one tower on the West
Wing and two entrances to either side of
the carriage porch. An interesting addition was the false gable between the
towers, a form Renwick also used on his
Romanesque Church of the Puritans in
New York City [Fig. 165].

Because of this reduction of the design,
Renwick was faced with the challenge of
fitting all the program's requirements into
two thirds of the space. As a result, the
interior plan was much altered. The sec-
ond-level museum floor remained undis-
turbed, but the third-floor gallery of art
was moved to the West Wing, where it
could retain the skylights that the Building Committee had specified. The library

space in the lower half of the Main Building was reduced to accommodate the large
lecture hall formerly in the West Wing.

21. James Renwick, Jr., Smithsonian Building, South Facade, rendering, painted by Louis Townsend and drawn by H. C. Moore, June 1848. Smithsonian Institution Archives, color slide in the Collection of the Office of Architectural History and Historic Preservation.

James Renwick, Jr., became an architect by observation and education. Through his father, an architectural amateur who had proposed a collegiate Gothic building as early as 1813, and through other members of the family, he had generous exposure to architecture and the other arts. As a student at Columbia College between 1831 and 1836, he received an education in science and engineering. Although he had little firsthand experience with the craft, his early buildings—such as Grace Church, Calvary Church, and the Smithsonian Building—were unusually sure in the use of materials and bold in the mixture of design elements. His use of the Gothic Revival at Grace and Calvary churches was sophisticated in successfully combining continental and British forms.[24] For the Smithsonian Building, he integrated German Romanesque sources for the design of the east entrance doors, the west cloister, and several towers with the English collegiate model for massing, and he used Norman moldings for decorative detail. Examining Renwick's specifications for the building, Regent William J. Hough stated that he found "them elaborately and minutely drawn, both in reference to detail of the work and permanence and durability of the structure."[25]

22. Portrait of James Renwick, Jr., holding his plans for St. Patrick's Cathedral, photograph of a painting by John Whetten Ehninger, 1853. Avery Architectural and Fine Arts Library, Columbia University in the City of New York.

23. Smithsonian Building, North Facade, photograph, 1858.

Smithsonian Institution, neg. 05456.

In midnineteenth-century Washington, the Smithsonian Building was distinctive in its physical elements: a horizontal linear mass punctuated by numerous vertical accents, the whole in a deep red-colored stone. Although its motifs and details were technically Romanesque, it owed very little to the massive walls and heavy, roughly articulated forms of traditional Norman architecture. The building's rhythmic linear massing flowed on each side from a dominant central block through low connectors to wings. While the east and west wings balanced each other, they were far from identical: one a rectangular block with battlements and chimneys, descending to an entrance porch on the east end, the other resembling a chapel with a projecting apse. Carrying the contrast to a finer level, the two cloistered walkways on the north facade were strongly dissimilar.

Heightening the building's picturesque quality was the impression of asymmetry created by the nine architecturally diverse towers. The central motif was twin towered: one tower short and finished with a pointed roof, the other taller, changing almost imperceptibly from square at the base to octagonal. Marking the point at which this flag tower became octagonal were four pepper-pot pinnacles. The campanile and two additional towers, including one at the northwest corner, brought the Mall facade to a total of five. All the towers housed necessary functional spaces and enhanced the building's silhouette by accenting its horizontal mass.[26]

In striking contrast to the north facade, the south of the building was dominated by a massive, square battlemented central tower with an attached octagonal stair tower rising well above it. The tower was divided into three sections, punctuated by a grand round-arched door on the first floor, a projecting oriel window on the second, and an elongated version of the windows in the East Wing on the third. Two other towers—one octagonal staircase tower and one square elevator tower for freight—contributed to the asymmetry of the south facade.

Constructed of red sandstone quarried in Seneca, Maryland, this dramatic building was unique not only in style but in material. As several building materials were under consideration in early 1847, the building might have been of light-colored marble, gray granite, or tawny sandstone. Its richly tinted stone was chosen by weighing studies conducted by David Dale Owen, in his role as geologist, and Charles Page, a physical scientist who reported on durability, with such aesthetic considerations as the visibility of shadows and detail and suitability for the medieval style.[27]

24. Smithsonian Building, South Facade, photograph, 1858–64.
Smithsonian Institution, neg. 36881.

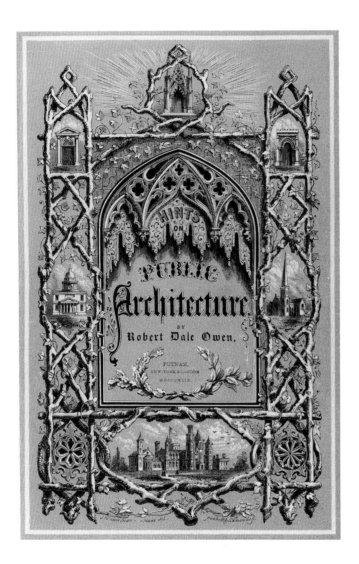

**25. James Renwick, Jr., wood
engraving, frontispiece from
Robert Dale Owen, *Hints on Public
Architecture*, 1849.** Smithsonian
Institution, neg. MNH 2534-J.

The building was grounded in its own
philosophical theory, explicated in a book
of considerable intellectual power. Authorized by the Board of Regents in 1846
as a description of the plan and architectural style, this book was *Hints on Public
Architecture*. In the hands of its author,
Robert Dale Owen, *Hints* became a treatise on the appropriate architectural expression of purpose in public buildings.[28]
Owen's cogent argument for the Smithsonian's medieval revival style made a
strong appeal to the intellect. His language, concept, and examples were drawn
from the work of the widely influential
John Claudius Loudon, who based his architectural principles on the theory of
Scottish Common Sense philosophers of
the eighteenth century.

Having established Loudon's architectural principles for the use of forms expressive of function, Owen argued that,
beginning with a well-grounded, functional plan, a good designer could find in
the numerous medieval styles an architectural expression suitable to the character
and fitness of the structure.[29] As further
evidence, Owen added cost-related statistics. His impressively detailed comparison of the costs per cubic foot of major
public buildings, such as the Treasury
Building and the Patent Office, with those
of the Smithsonian Building sought to
show how cost effective the medieval revival style was.[30]

**26. "Smithsonian Institute,"
lithograph by Edward Sachse &
Co., ca. 1855–60.** Collection of the
Office of Architectural History and Historic
Preservation, Smithsonian Institution,
neg. 93-2053.

The medieval revival style was chosen for its expression of the American character and its association with collegiate institutions. Owen defined the character of the nation in terms such as vigor, flexibility, independence, and practical economy. These characteristics he translated into flexible space use, picturesque silhouette, and practical use of native materials, all of which he contended could be ascribed only to medieval architecture.[31] He concluded that the Smithsonian Building design had the qualities deserving "to be named as a National Style of Architecture for America."[32] Also inherent in the medieval style and in the linear massing of the Smithsonian Building was an association with the traditional English college. That Owen intended the Smithsonian Building to be read as a collegiate building was apparent in his own statement:

nor do I believe that any one, of moderately cultivated taste, in looking upon that building, would mistake its character, or connect it, in his mind, with other than a scientific or collegiate foundation.[33]

27. James Renwick, Jr., Octagonal Tower, wood engraving, from Robert Dale Owen, *Hints on Public Architecture*, 1849. Smithsonian Institution, neg. MNH 2534-F.

28. James Renwick, Jr., West Wing, wood engraving by Childs, from Robert Dale Owen, *Hints on Public Architecture*, 1849. Smithsonian Institution, neg. MNH 2534-D.

The potency of *Hints on Public Architecture* lay in its combination of the visual images, the persuasive argument, and Owen's frequently poetic language. These elements were expressions of the aesthetic that characterized both Renwick and Owen. When it was published in 1849, *Hints on Public Architecture* was adorned with a series of eight engravings of Renwick drawings illustrating aspects of the building, nine additional views by other artists, and renderings of several other Renwick buildings. A close collaboration between Robert Dale Owen and James Renwick, Jr., was apparent, based on a shared belief in an architecture that was historically informed but not doctrinaire.

29. James Renwick, Jr., Southern Gateway, wood engraving by Bobbett & Edmonds, from Robert Dale Owen, *Hints on Public Architecture*, 1849. Smithsonian Institution, neg. MNH 2534-G.

Hints on Public Architecture set the Smithsonian Building apart as the embodiment of an aesthetic philosophy. In the correspondence of the Owen brothers, the emphasis had already been on evolving a plan that suited the multiple functions that the building would serve. Additionally, Robert Mills and both Owen brothers had selected the medieval revival style and certain architectural forms for their expressive power. As a result of this predetermined design approach, the choice of architect and the evolution of the design led to a building that symbolized an idea as well as housed an institution.

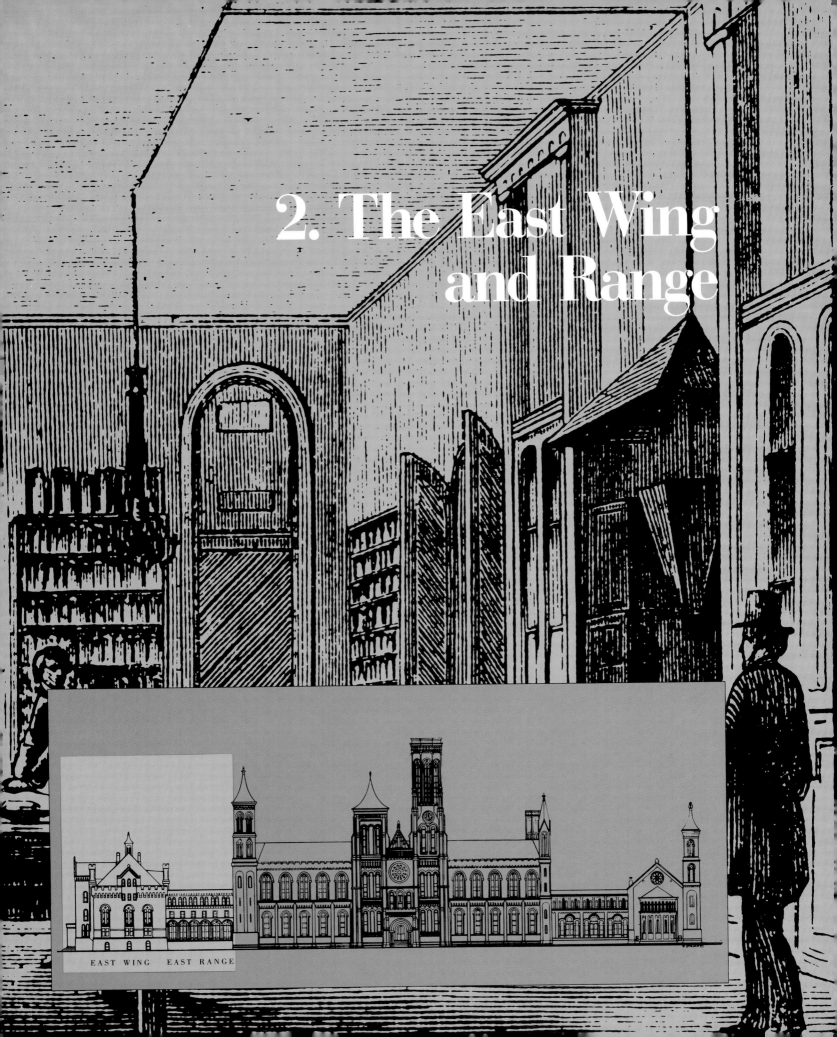

2. The East Wing and Range

EAST WING   EAST RANGE

*T*he East Wing and Range were the first portions of the Smithsonian Building to be completed. For over a year, all the functions of the fledgling Institution were carried on within their walls: there was an office for the Secretary and one for the Librarian, a lecture hall, two laboratories, and an apparatus room. Adjustments to the ill-suited space were constant in the first few years, while the concept of the Institution was redefined by the forceful first Secretary. Joseph Henry made significant changes to adapt the East Wing to the purposes of a budding research institution rather than a public teaching college. As the Smithsonian Building was gradually completed, the myriad functions housed in the East Wing and Range were dispersed.

The role of the East Wing took a dramatic turn with the introduction in 1855 of domestic quarters for the first Secretary and his family. From the rooms directly beneath the Henry apartments, the International Exchange Service disseminated scientific publications to scholarly institutions both in the United States and abroad. The East Range continued to house laboratories until 1872, when Henry designated it the administrative headquarters of the Smithsonian.

When Spencer Baird succeeded Henry as Secretary, he oversaw the renovation of this end of the building for expanded administrative functions. The danger of fire to the administrative heart of the Smithsonian inspired in 1884 the complete renovation of the east end, which provided not only a fireproof structure but also several additional floors. Into modern times the East Wing and Range have served as the seat of the Secretaries. Special projects, including the Art Room and the Smithsonian Institution Archives, as well as the Secretary's Parlor (later called the Meeting Room), have been housed in the East Wing.

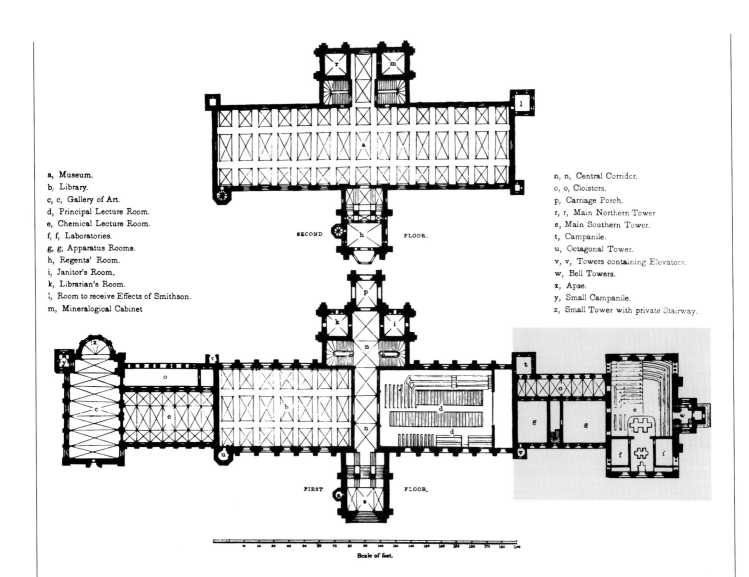

a, Museum.
b, Library.
c, c, Gallery of Art.
d, Principal Lecture Room.
e, Chemical Lecture Room.
f, f, Laboratories.
g, g, Apparatus Rooms.
h, Regents' Room.
i, Janitor's Room.
k, Librarian's Room.
l, Room to receive Effects of Smithson.
m, Mineralogical Cabinet

n, n, Central Corridor.
o, o, Cloisters.
p, Carriage Porch.
r, r, Main Northern Tower
s, Main Southern Tower.
t, Campanile.
u, Octagonal Tower.
v, v, Towers containing Elevators.
w, Bell Towers.
x, Apse.
y, Small Campanile.
z, Small Tower with private Stairway.

SECOND FLOOR.

FIRST FLOOR.

Scale of feet.

30. James Renwick, Jr., Floor Plan, detail of the East Wing and Range, wood engraving by J. H. Hall from *Hints on Public Architecture*, 1849. Smithsonian Institution, neg. 92-15757.

David Dale Owen proposed a particular type of lecture theater, designed to enable the speaker to illustrate his points with scientific demonstrations. Capable of holding 300 to 400 people in sharply banked seats and a gallery, the hall was small enough for all viewers to see the experiments.[1] The podium contained a very large double-cross table for displaying objects or conducting experiments. Be-

hind the podium was a laboratory divided into three compartments, the central of which could be opened to the lecture hall. This unusual form reflected the Owen brothers' belief that an environment of combined demonstration and oration promoted learning.[2]

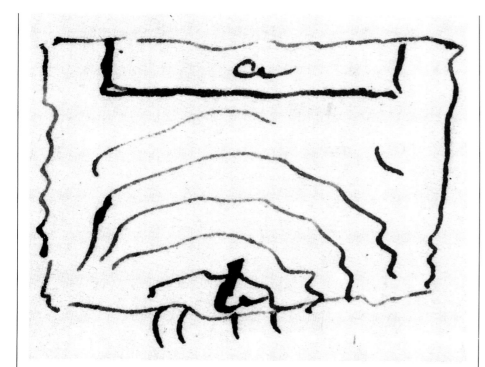

31. Joseph Henry, New Lecture Room, drawing from *Desk Diary of 1849*, May 16. Smithsonian Institution Archives, Smithsonian Institution, neg. 92-16513.

Joseph Henry's very different concept of the purpose of the Institution, which did not include the interactive educational purpose for which the Owen lecture hall had been designed, led him to find numerous problems with the East Wing lecture hall, including poor lighting and ventilation, and overcrowding. After making temporary adjustments to the lighting and seating,[3] Henry undertook the redesign of the hall. In his desk diary he sketched a plan that showed the lecturer in the center, the focus of curved, tiered seating. Only a year after the East Wing had been completed, the entire interior was gutted to accommodate Henry's new hall. Rising two stories to a vaulted ceiling, it seated almost 1,000 people.[4]

Separated from the lecture hall for fire safety by a thick wall and iron door, the Chemical Laboratory [Fig. 32] and the Laboratory of Natural History [Fig. 33] were located from 1849 to 1872 in adjoining rooms on the first floor of the East Range.[5] The slender, clustered columns with carved capitals and the round-arched doors and windows of these two rooms echoed James Renwick, Jr.'s exterior details. Rounded forms for doors and windows were thought to harmonize better with a flat ceiling than the pointed Gothic arch.[6] The Chemical Laboratory was used by qualified professionals, while the Laboratory of Natural History was open for study of natural history specimens. Research resulting from the use of the laboratories was to be published in the Smithsonian's *Contributions to Knowledge.*[7]

Upon his appointment as Secretary in December 1846, Joseph Henry had been promised a yearly salary of $3,500 and lodgings. Almost a decade later, however, he and his family still lived in temporary, rented accommodations close to the Smithsonian Building.[8] The construction in 1855 of a second-floor suite of rooms where the lecture hall had been remedied the arrangement. The East Range laboratories and workrooms proved a constant source of annoyance for Henry and his family because of the foul odors seeping into the living quarters.[9] Despite these fumes, Henry was generally pleased with his living situation, stating, "we have very pleasant and commodious apartments in the Smithsonian building."[10]

32. Chemical Laboratory, woodcut from William J. Rhees, *An Account of the Smithsonian Institution . . . , ca. 1856.* Smithsonian Institution, neg. 43804-E.

33. Laboratory of Natural History, woodcut from William J. Rhees, *An Account of the Smithsonian Institution . . . , ca. 1856.*

Smithsonian Institution, neg. 43804-F.

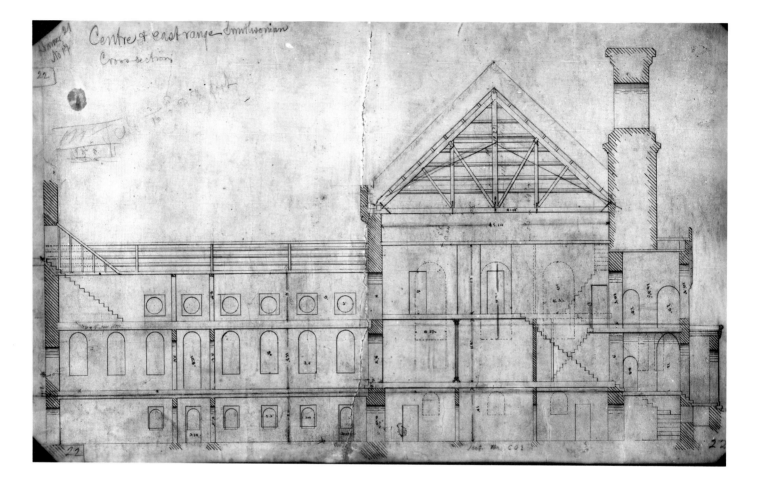

34. Section through East Wing and Range, drawing, 1855.

Smithsonian Institution Archives, Smithsonian Institution, neg. 89-10064.

This cutaway drawing was created for the insertion of apartments into the East Wing for the Henry family. When the lecture hall was removed in 1855, its lofty space was divided into two floors. On the upper level, living quarters were established; the lower area was arranged as a large single room for the storage and distribution of books.[11] A long, steep staircase descended from the Henry apartments to the east door. In 1871 Henry recorded:

Sad accident happened at about half past eleven to Mrs. Henry. . . . I heard a loud crash and called to Mrs. H. to know what it was but receiving no answer the idea occurred to me that she had fallen down the stairs.[12]

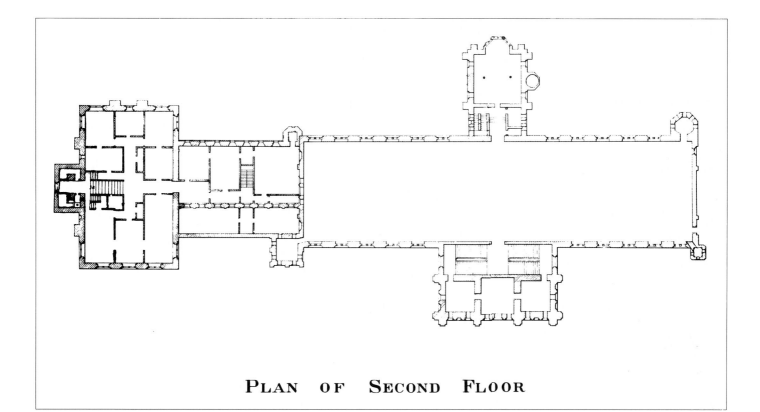

PLAN   OF   SECOND   FLOOR

35. Floor Plan of the second floor of the East Wing, drawing by Gorham, 1879. Smithsonian Institution Archives, Smithsonian Institution, neg. 1296.

The Henry apartments consisted of eight main rooms, including a music room, a parlor, a dining room, two bedrooms, and Joseph Henry's private study.[13] A series of photographs of the three main rooms were taken by Henry's personal friend, the artist Titian R. Peale. This series can be dated to the summer of 1862 on the basis of an inscription on the back of one photo-graph in the collection of the Smithsonian's Office of Architectural History.[14]

The three rooms photographed by Peale were those used for the reception and entertainment of visitors and were lo-cated along the northern side of the suite. The dining room, the parlor, and the mu-sic room were carpeted throughout, as were such rooms in many houses of the mid–nineteenth century. The floral carpet chosen appears to have been a Brussels carpet, a type preferred by wealthier households.[15] Since curtains were little used during the summer months, the car-pets and fabrics in these rooms were shaded from the sun's rays by interior "shutter-blinds."[16] Lighting in the suite was provided by gas chandeliers, then called "gaseliers."[17]

Henry's furniture was an eclectic mix, ranging from "Grecian" and Gothic-style pieces in the dining room [Fig. 36] to Ro-coco Revival and wicker furniture in the parlor [Fig. 37] and music room [Figs. 38 and 39]. The small Gothic side chair in the left corner of the Henry dining room closely resembles the armchairs designed by James Renwick, Jr., for use in the Re-

36. Dining Room of the Henry apartments, photograph by Titian R. Peale, 1862. Smithsonian Institution, neg. 3251.

37. Parlor of the Henry apartments, photograph by Titian R. Peale, 1862. Smithsonian Institution, neg. 3253.

of Washington from the top of a clothes press. She was shutting the door of the press, when the bust came down, — cut her temple and broke in one of the side bones of her nose.[19]

39. Music Room of the Henry apartments, photograph by Titian R. Peale, 1862. Collection of the Office of Architectural History and Historic Preservation, Smithsonian Institution, neg. 46638-C.

38. Music Room of the Henry apartments, photograph by Titian R. Peale, 1862. Smithsonian Institution, neg. 3252.

gents' Room [Fig. 154]. This side chair, along with the Gothic Revival high-back chair at the table and the tall Gothic secretary desk against the wall, constitute the only pieces of furniture visible that harmonized with the architectural style of the building. The upholstery of the chairs and sofas was protected from sun and soil by fitted slipcovers, which were probably removed for more formal entertaining.[18] The bust of George Washington, visible in the music room, was the topic of one of Henry's letters:

We are all well except Mary, who met with an accident, in the falling on her head of a bust

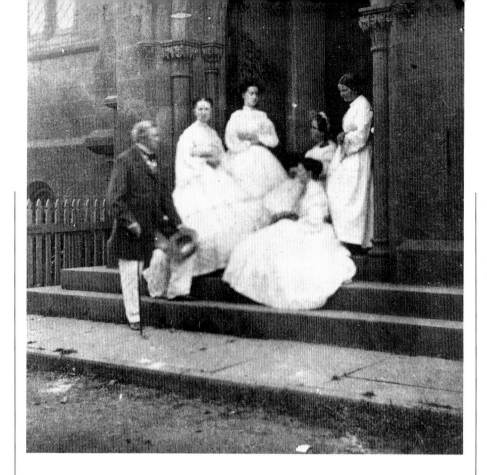

40. Henry family at the East Door of the Smithsonian Building, photograph, ca. 1862. Smithsonian Institution Archives, neg. SA-203.

Henry and his family posed at the door to their apartments on a summer day in the midst of the Civil War. The apartments were the scene of many festivities since distinguished guests who attended Smithsonian lectures and meetings were frequently entertained in the family quarters.[20] Henry's family continued to use the East Wing as their residence until his death in 1878.

■

Shortly after Henry's death the apartments were again photographed. This later set of stereo views documented the private rooms, the two bedrooms and Henry's study, which were located on the south side of the East Wing. Only the photograph of Henry's bedroom reveals the event that had just occurred. The chairs were arranged around the deathbed, while medicine bottles and other articles associated with illness were set on the small table at the foot of the bed.[21]

Henry's bedroom furniture, like that of the parlor, dining room, and music room, represented a mix of periods and styles. The Renaissance Revival bureau and sofa, the Rococo Revival armchair, the so-called French bedstead,[22] the Empire-style side chairs, and two plain rocking chairs of no particular style were grouped together on a floral medallion rug. Light was supplied by two gas fixtures: a rod-type suspension chandelier with three arms and a center light dating from the 1870s, and a hinged wall bracket over the bed.[23] The marble-topped radiator in the corner was one of several in the apartments.[24]

■

The second bedroom in the Henry suite was in the southwest corner of the wing. Although furnished similarly to Henry's bedroom, the room retained its original 1850s gas chandelier. The most unusual piece of furniture in the room was the simple but elegant folding chair, of a type introduced by Michael Thonet's bentwood furniture factory in Vienna in 1866.[25] The presence of this chair suggests that the photograph was taken after 1873, when the Thonet company opened a branch in New York City, greatly expanding the popularity of this furniture throughout the country.[26]

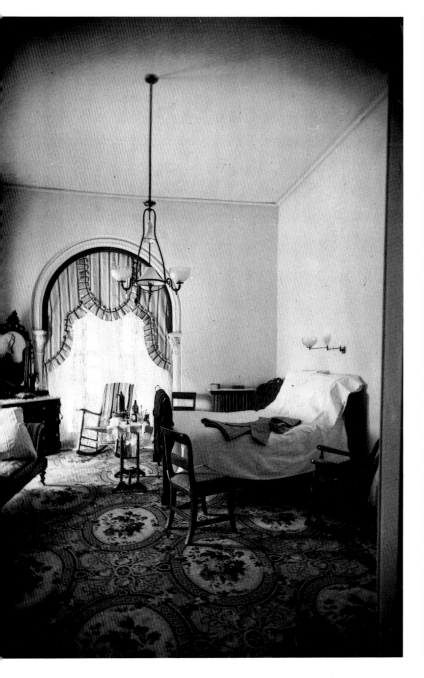

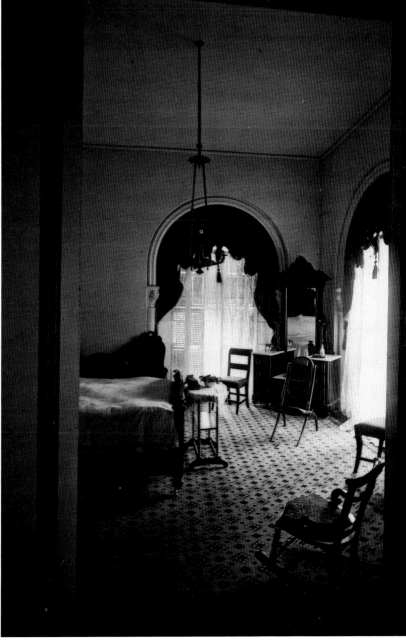

41. Joseph Henry's Bedroom in the Henry apartments, photograph by Thomas W. Smillie, ca. 1878.
Smithsonian Institution, neg. 1240.

42. Bedroom in the Henry apartments, photograph by Thomas W. Smillie, ca. 1878.
Smithsonian Institution, neg. 1238.

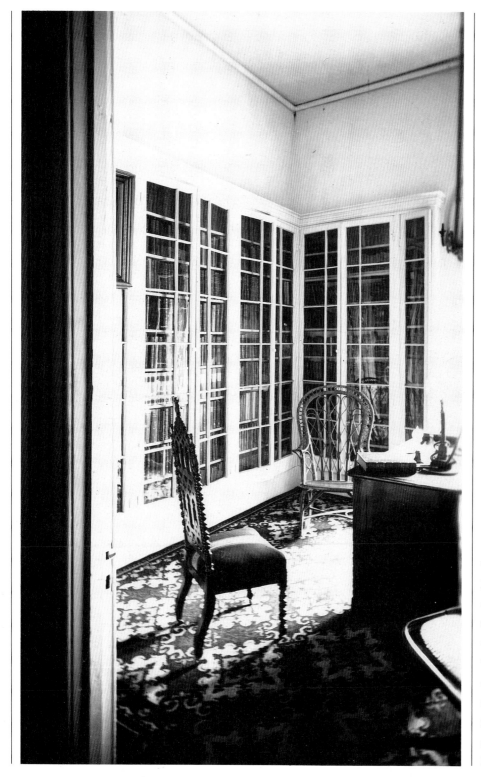

43. Joseph Henry's Study in the Henry apartments, photograph by Thomas W. Smillie, ca. 1878.
Smithsonian Institution, neg. 1236.

Joseph Henry's private study in the apartments occupied a small room between the two bedrooms on the south side. Late in 1862, Henry's only son, William, died of cholera in the East Wing apartments. A touching entry in Mary's diary for New Year's Day 1863 made reference to the room and to her family's loss:

We watched the old year out and the new year in. Nell and I sat in Father's study until the heavy boom of a cannon told us the old year was dead. I shall not soon forget that sound[;] it was the last of the year that knew our Will.[27]

44. Mary Henry's Studio in the East Range, photograph by Thomas W. Smillie, ca. 1878.
Smithsonian Institution, neg. 1237.

Mary Henry worked in this artist's studio on the second floor of the East Range, adjoining the Henry living quarters. The elongated atelier, effectively lit by two skylights, also had a row of portal windows. These portals, which originally provided light to the East Range from the open cloistered walkway on the north side, remained in the wall after the cloister was enclosed in 1858.[28] By her own admission, Mary Henry was not a particularly gifted artist; she worked for six to

eight years to complete a clay bust of her father before turning to painting.[29] By 1871 she was taking painting lessons at Theodore Kauffman's school in Washington.[30] In this view of her studio, six easels were set up amid still lifes and props, suggesting a class or a group working together. Two of these "props" are notable: one, a chair designed by James Renwick, Jr., for the Regents' Room, which can also be seen in the background of one of the paintings, and a large plaster bust of Apollo, which came to the Smithsonian in 1858 as part of the collections of the defunct National Institute [Fig. 154 and Fig. 115]. Both chair and bust remain in the building as part of its furniture collection.

45. John H. Richard's Studio in the East Range, photograph, ca. 1879. Smithsonian Institution, neg. 92-3861.

After Henry's death in 1878, the family left the apartments. The rooms of the East Wing were used as offices, and the artist's studio in the Range was given over to John H. Richard, a French-born scientific illustrator. Richard began his connection with the Smithsonian in 1855, painting illustrations of fish, reptiles, and amphibians for the reports of several government exploring expeditions, including the Wilkes Expedition. Although he left the Smithsonian for a time in the 1860s and early 1870s, he returned in 1875 to prepare specimens for the 1876 Centennial Exhibition in Philadelphia. Here, approximately a year before his death, Richard was painting fish casts for the Berlin International Fishery Exhibition of 1880. The Smithsonian received the grand prize of a silver gilt vase for the fishery exhibition, which featured Richard's work.[31]

46. Spencer Baird's Office in the East Range, photograph by Thomas W. Smillie, ca. 1878.

Smithsonian Institution, neg. 2337.

This room, previously the Laboratory of Natural History, had been converted to administrative offices in 1872, when Joseph Henry removed all museum functions from the East Wing and Range. It was Henry's long-held belief that the Smithsonian Institution and the National Museum should be distinct entities.[32] He hoped both to "show how small a space is sufficient to carry on the legitimate operations of the establishment" and to remove the source of bad odors that permeated his living quarters.[33]

While serving the Smithsonian as Assistant Secretary, Spencer Baird had ordered a special desk from the Wooten

Desk Company in Indianapolis.[34] First patented in 1874 by William S. Wooten, this innovative desk, visible on the left, provided a filing system with pigeonholes and writing surfaces. Popular in the late nineteenth century, it was advertised as combining "neatness, system and order," with "every particle of space practically utilized."[35] Baird and his assistants had their offices on the first floor of the East Range until 1879, when the Henry apartments were occupied for office use.[36]

Transforming the Henry apartments into offices in 1879 greatly increased the amount of space afforded to the Institution's operations. These rooms, however, were considered highly combustible and insecure. The architectural firm of Cluss & Schulze presented plans for fireproofing this section of the building. They contemplated dramatic changes to the interior without significantly altering the architectural appearance of the building.[37]

In addition to the new offices of the Secretary and his assistants, the renovated East Wing and Range contained the International Exchange Service, the Registrar's office, the Chief Clerk's office, and the office of the Librarian. Other uses included a post office, a library and reading room, the archives, several rooms for laboratories, and the National Academy of Sciences.[38]

47. South facade of the East Wing, photograph, ca. 1883. Smithsonian Institution, neg. 86-11899.

Comparison of the architect's drawing with a photograph dated around 1883 shows how Cluss & Schulze effectively doubled the available space in the building while minimizing exterior alterations. They removed James Renwick, Jr.'s "postern door" [Fig. 47], which had provided direct access to the lecture hall and later to the International Exchange offices, and inserted a suite of rooms above the crenel-lation. Four floors were created where there had been only two, and in the East Range three full-height levels were created. To accomplish this transformation of interior space while maintaining the building's architectural character, Cluss reused much of the Seneca sandstone removed during reconstruction, retaining most of the original decorative detail.[39]

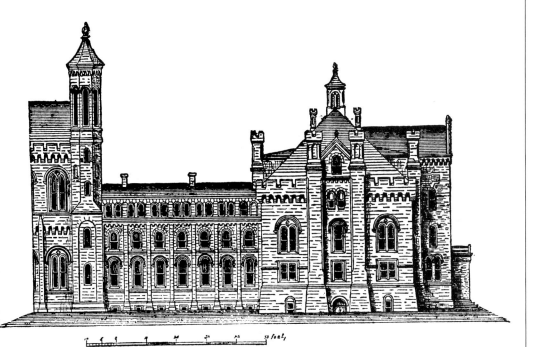

48. Adolf Cluss, South Elevation of the East Wing, drawing, 1884. Smithsonian Institution, neg. 89-8554.

49. Floor Plan of the second floor of the East Wing and Range, drawing, 1884. Smithsonian Institution Archives, Smithsonian Institution, neg. 2533.

In designing the layout of the second floor for the 1884 renovation, Cluss & Schulze closely followed the arrangement of rooms in Henry's time. The major changes involved replacing and moving the stairwell. The layout of the basement and the first and third floors followed the configuration of the second floor, while the rooms of the fourth floor were smaller because of their position under the roof gables.

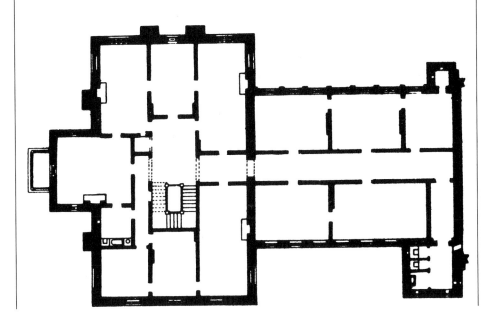

After the 1884 renovation, the Smithsonian Institution International Exchange Service again occupied offices on the first floor. Established in 1848, this organization facilitated the exchange of scientific publications among American and foreign institutions, government departments, societies, and individuals around the world.[40] In 1855 the first-floor room of the wing had been set aside as a depository for extra copies of Smithsonian publications and for the reception and distribution of all articles of exchange.[41] After the postern door was removed, the freight functions were carried out from the basement. "Exchanges" employees unloaded wooden boxes into the basement, where a freight lift had been constructed in 1884 [Fig. 50]. The offices and packing rooms of the Exchanges remained little changed until 1893.

The doorway of the east end appeared unaltered from the days of Joseph Henry, despite the total renovation of 1884. Posing on the steps of the east entrance, where thirty years earlier the Henry family had stood for their photograph, the fourteen staff members of the International Exchange Service in 1892 showed the growth of the services provided by the Institution [Fig. 51]. By 1891 the cost of the Exchanges to the Smithsonian in space and salary had become a considerable burden.[42]

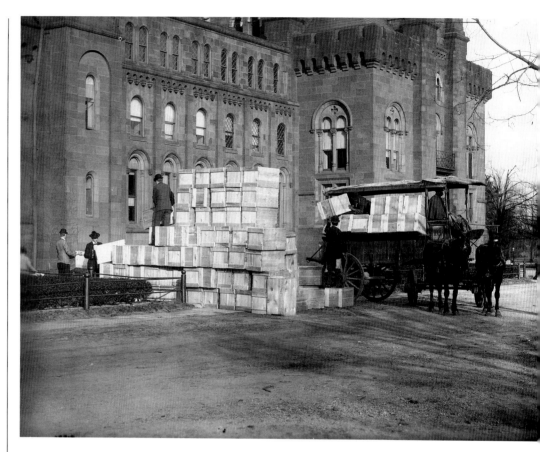

50. Deliveries to the International Exchange Service, south facade of the East Wing, photograph, ca. 1910. Smithsonian Institution, neg. 13318.

51. The staff of the International Exchange Service, East Wing, photograph, 1891. Smithsonian Institution, neg. 82-3382.

52. International Exchange Office in the basement of the East Wing, photograph, ca. 1910. Smithsonian Institution, neg. 82-3217.

In 1893 all the Exchanges offices on the first floor were relocated to the basement of the East Wing and Range, freeing up valuable office space.[43] In order better to accommodate the offices, Secretary Samuel Langley directed the Architect of the Capitol, Edward Clark, with whom the Smithsonian consulted on architectural matters, to make alterations to the basement.[44] Part of a suite of five rooms, the room seen here was used for preparing packages for distribution to institutions around the world. Owing to the rapid increase of the work of the Exchanges, the need for more space was expected almost as soon as these rooms were occupied. The International Exchange Service, which grew to fill much of the basement, remained in the building until 1966.[45]

53. Publications Office on the second floor of the East Range, photograph, 1914. Smithsonian Institution, neg. 82-3378.

The removal of the Exchanges to the basement allowed the main floors of the East Wing and Range to be dedicated entirely to office use. In 1914 a series of photographs taken by the Smithsonian's resident photographer, Thomas W. Smillie, captured a day in the working life of the Institution.

These offices on the second floor of the East Range diverged widely in their conveniences and conditions. The quarters for the publications staff [Fig. 53] appear to have been crowded. As walls lacked

54. Appointments Clerk's Office on the second floor of the East Range, photograph, 1914. Smithsonian Institution, neg. 82-3222.

electrical sockets, additional lamps were plugged into the chandelier, which provided both gas and electric power as insurance against interruptions to the electric service.[46] The Appointments Clerk's more spacious office was also lighted by a combination fixture [Fig. 54]. On the desk was a telephone; as early as 1881 thirty phones had been installed in offices in the Smithsonian and National Museum buildings.[47] In the Chief Clerk's office, a modern electric fixture, capable of providing better light at a lower cost, replaced the outdated combination chandeliers [Fig. 55].[48] These offices serve much the same capacity today as they did in 1914.

55. Chief Clerk's Office on the second floor of the East Wing, photograph, 1914. Smithsonian Institution, neg. 82-3218.

56. Secretary's Office on the second floor of the East Wing, photograph, 1972. Smithsonian Institution, neg. 72-4893.

The Chief Clerk's room continued throughout the twentieth century to be used as support space for the Secretary, whose office was in the adjacent room, once Joseph Henry's bedroom. In 1964, at the request of S. Dillon Ripley, then newly appointed Secretary, the Institution began to restore the interior of the Smithsonian Building. Although the exterior had not been altered since the 1884 reconstruction, the appearance of the interior had changed considerably in the name of modernization. Green linoleum covered the wood floors, fluorescent lighting fixtures had replaced the gas chandeliers, and drab metal desks and file cabinets furnished the offices.

These two photographs from the 1970s

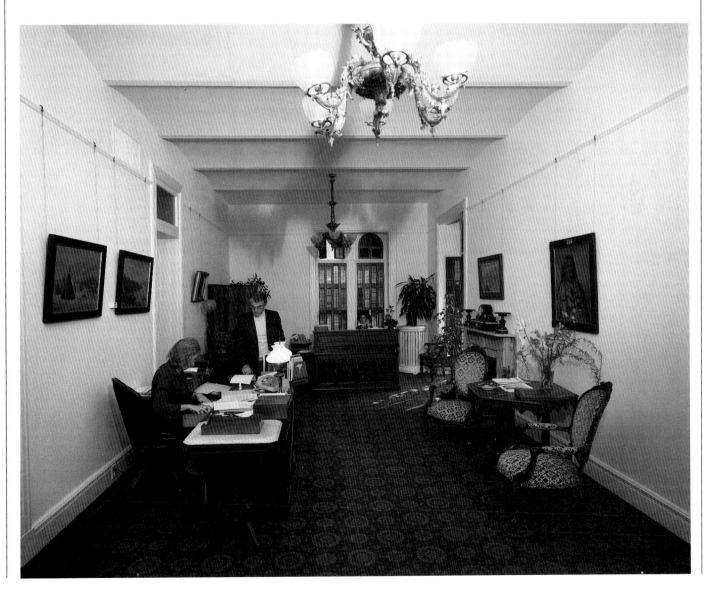

57. Secretary's Reception Office on the second floor of the East Wing, photograph, 1976. Smithsonian Institution, neg. 76-4136.

show the Secretary's office and his reception office, furnished with nineteenth-century furniture and works of art on loan from the Smithsonian's National Collection of Fine Arts (now the National Museum of American Art). The furnishings reflected an effort to create a period ambience befitting the architecture. Some objects, such as the bust of Joel Poinsett [Fig. 56] and the paintings by George Catlin [Fig. 57], recalled the earlier days of the Institution, when they had been on exhibit in the building.

Not all the rooms of the East Wing were used as offices; some fulfilled very specialized functions. The seed was planted for the growth of the Smithsonian's art museums when in 1900 Secretary Samuel Langley transformed one of the second-floor rooms into the "Art Room" for the study of prints. Likewise, the forerunner of the Smithsonian Institution Archives was established in a top-floor room under the gables in 1894. In the room that has come to serve as the Secretary's Meeting Room, the Smithsonian Regents held their meetings for the first seventy years of the twentieth century.

The Art Room was established in what had been the Henrys' music room [Fig. 38]. Secretary Langley declared to the Regents that

the scientific side of the Institution's activities has been in the past so much greater than its aesthetic that it is well to recall the undoubted fact that it was intended by Congress to be a curator of the national art, and that this function has never been forgotten, though often in abeyance.[49]

The room was expressly designed to reflect the aesthetic tradition evoked by Langley through reference to great works

58. The Art Room on the second floor of the East Range, photograph, ca. 1903. Smithsonian Institution, neg. 82-3355.

in the history of Western art. Encircling it was a plaster frieze copied from the world-famous frieze of the Parthenon, in this day unequivocally the acme of classical art history. Carbon photographs by Adolphe Braun introduced portraits and paintings by the great masters of the Renaissance, another high point of Western art history.[50] The furnishings were specially designed by the architectural firm of Hornblower & Marshall for this location. One intriguing adaptation was an elaborate system of hardware that enabled the drawers of the print file cabinets to be raised to an almost vertical position for viewing prints.[51] The golden oak table in the center of the room and the oak armchair to its left were intended for visitors looking at prints or using reference books.

59. Under Secretary's Office on the second floor of the East Range, photograph by Richard Strauss, 1992. Smithsonian Institution, neg. 92-16572.

Partial restoration of the Art Room was begun in 1990 with the return of the Hornblower & Marshall table and three of the original chairs. Although the room is now used as the office of the Institution's Under Secretary, the spirit of the Art Room has been evoked by several paintings from the National Museum of American Art.[52] Other furnishings of similar style and material were added. Although not the original pieces, the oak flat file and the chairs around the table recall those in the Art Room of 1903.

60. Smithsonian Archives on the fourth floor of the East Wing, photograph, ca. 1900. Smithsonian Institution, neg. 13406.

In 1894 a room on the fourth floor of the East Wing was converted for use as the Smithsonian Institution Archives.[53] It was furnished with walnut cabinets for the storage of early manuscripts and correspondence as well as drawings, photographs, and plans of the Institution. Over a large worktable in the center of the room, a combination gas-electric chande- lier was hung from the pressed tin ceiling. Beneath the two framed pictures to the right of the door can be seen the mouth- piece of an "oral annunciator," an early type of intercom installed throughout the East Wing in 1884.[54]

61. Law Library on the fourth floor of the East Wing, photograph by Colin Varga, 1987. Smithsonian Institution, neg. 87-4894-3.

Today the former Archives Room is used as a meeting room and law library by the Smithsonian's General Counsel. Although the cabinets and tin ceiling remain, the chandelier has been replaced by two electrified gas fixtures, and the "Harvard" stove has long since been removed. In 1913, coinciding with a major reorganization of the material in the Archives, the wooden panels in the doors of the cases were replaced by glass to enable the contents to be seen without opening the doors.[55]

62. Presentation of the bust of Alexander Graham Bell in the Regents' Room on the second floor of the East Wing, photograph, 1926. Smithsonian Institution, neg. 82-3348.

This photograph was taken at the unveiling of a bust of Alexander Graham Bell in 1926, when this room over the east entrance served as the Regents' Room. Bell, widely known for his invention of the telephone, was an important figure in the history of the Smithsonian. Serving diligently on the Board of Regents from 1898 to 1922, he was instrumental in bringing James Smithson's remains to the United States in 1904.[56] Important national figures were present at the unveiling, including then Chief Justice of the Supreme Court and the twenty-seventh President of the United States, William H. Taft; Charles G. Dawes, then Vice President; and the Secretary of the Smithsonian, Charles D. Walcott.[57] The participants were seated at a table expressly designed for the Regents' Room by Hornblower & Marshall. Paintings, prints, and ceramics representing the range of the Smithsonian's art holdings enhanced the setting.

63. Certificate of Achievement Award in the Regents' Room, photograph, 1963. Smithsonian Institution, neg. 63387.

The decor of the Regents' Room in 1963 evidenced a renewed interest in using period furnishings and in reviving the history of the Institution. The presence of the first Secretaries of the Smithsonian, Joseph Henry and Spencer Baird, was felt at this awards ceremony through the portrait paintings. Historical embellishment began as early as the late 1920s, when the fireplace surround, of a delicate neoclassical style executed in white marble, was placed in the room. The table designed by Hornblower & Marshall was replaced by a late Victorian dining table, presaging the room's next use.

64. Secretary's Parlor, photograph, 1972. Smithsonian Institution, neg. 72-4891.

After the original Regents' Room in the South Tower was restored to use in 1970, this room became the Secretary's Parlor. In an effort to evoke the character of "James Renwick's delightful and entertaining Smithsonian castle on the Mall,"[58] Secretary S. Dillon Ripley selected an eclectic mix of nineteenth-century furnishings to decorate the East Wing's ceremonial rooms and offices. The domestic feeling of the Secretary's Parlor recalled Joseph Henry's dining room [Fig. 36]. Just as Henry's vision of a scholarly center at the Smithsonian was being reborn in the Upper Main Hall, the Henry family apartments provided inspiration for this restoration. Ripley explained:

I've restored Henry's rooms to something like their original decor, and we're in the process of similarly redecorating a dozen other rooms on this floor. I think the inside of the building ought to match its outside, at least as far as is practically possible.[59]

65. Secretary's Meeting Room on the second floor of the East Wing, photograph by Richard Strauss, 1992. Smithsonian Institution, neg. 92-16578.

In 1984, after the appointment of Robert McCormick Adams, this space became a meeting room for the Secretary. The Secretary's Meeting Room, as it was then renamed, expressed the comfortable American classical style of 1830–50. It was painted a shade of tan described by Andrew Jackson Downing as "fawn."[60] Classical references embellished the rather plain, massive furniture: slender columns, capitals, acanthus leaves, Ionic scrolls, and lion's paw feet. The signed secretary desk to the left of the window, made by Isaac Vose and Sons of Boston around 1820, was a rare example of furniture labeled by Vose from the period. On the other side of the window hung John Mix Stanley's *International Indian Council Held at Tahlequah Indian Territory in 1843*.[61] This oil painting was one of the few that survived the fire of 1865.

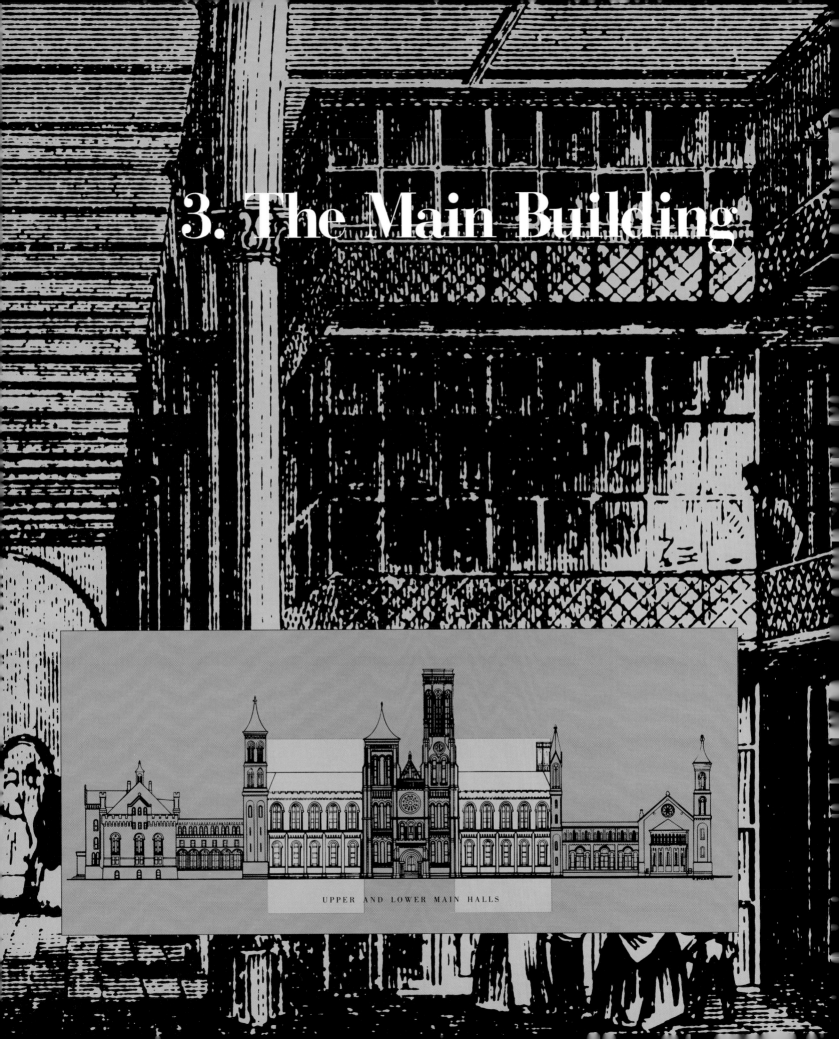

3. The Main Building

UPPER AND LOWER MAIN HALLS

*T*he story of the Smithsonian Building's Lower Main Hall reflects the chang-

The Lower Main Hall

ing relationship of the Institution to the public. Before the building was completed, the hall had been envisioned as a public library and a lecture hall. When
it was constructed, exhibits filled the space to overflowing. The vast array of
natural history specimens drew visitors and students to the National Museum.
From this one great room, the museum grew in scope and professionalism to fill
three new Smithsonian museum buildings, which were opened in 1881, 1911,
and 1964. Each of these buildings initiated a reconsideration of the role of the
Smithsonian Building's great space. With the erection of the first National Museum Building, the exhibition space was divided between curatorial and public
functions. The completion of the National Museum of Natural History signaled
the change of the hall to a library, with related Graphic Arts exhibits. The hall
was cleared in the 1960s, when the Graphic Arts exhibits were transferred to the
newly erected Museum of History and Technology (today known as the National
Museum of American History).

When Secretary Leonard Carmichael redefined the role of the museum in Cold
War America as that of a public information center, the scene was set for the
Lower Main Hall to serve as a focal point for the distribution of museum information. The name Great Hall was embraced during this time, suggesting not only
the building's identity as a castle but also its communal function.[1] Throughout
the 1960s and 1970s foreign dignitaries and heads of state were ceremoniously
received in this richly Victorian space, amid exhibits emphasizing the origins
and development of the Smithsonian and the city it inhabits. In the 1980s the
Great Hall became the official seat of the Visitor Information and Associates'
Reception Center, redecorated in a light, inviting color scheme and equipped
with the apparatus of an information age. This last transformation concretely
defined the Great Hall as the literal and symbolic heart of the Smithsonian.

The 1849 plan for the Smithsonian Building did not suit the goals of the Institution
as Secretary Joseph Henry saw them. This
large lecture hall, one of four that Robert
Dale Owen had suggested for the building, was abandoned by Henry when the
East Wing lecture room was enlarged in
1849–50. In place of the lecture hall on
the floor plan, Henry established a room
to house a collection of scientific instruments.[2] During construction, the interior
structure of this area collapsed. Henry recorded in his desk diary that

four men were working in the apparatus room
when they sensed the south east part of the
floor to begin to sink. They sprung to the door
leading into the Library part and miracu-
lously escaped injury. Prof. Jewett and his
wife . . . were alarmed by a large amount of
dust issuing from the door in the brick wall
and seeing the men tumble out over each
other at the same time a crash was heard in
the apparatus room.[3]

The accident spurred a reconsideration of
the building's construction method. An
investigation was conducted by three
outside experts: John R. Nierensee, a
well-known Austrian-trained architect
practicing in Baltimore; Colonel William
Turnbull of the U.S. Topographical Engineers; and Edward B. White, an architect
from Charleston, South Carolina. This
panel's report convinced the Regents to
adopt James Renwick, Jr.'s plan to fireproof the building, making it safe to house
collections.[4] By the time construction was
recommenced, Renwick had been replaced by Barton S. Alexander, an engi-

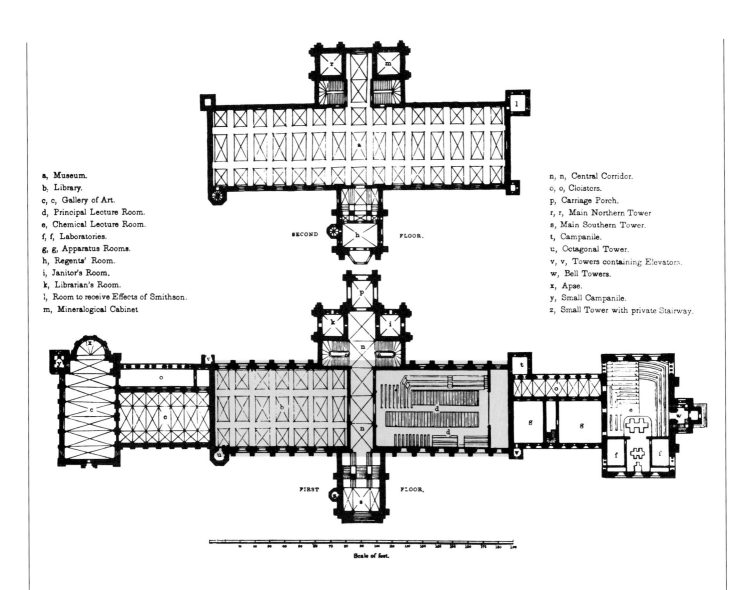

a, Museum.
b, Library.
c, c, Gallery of Art.
d, Principal Lecture Room.
e, Chemical Lecture Room.
f, f, Laboratories.
g, g, Apparatus Rooms.
h, Regents' Room.
i, Janitor's Room.
k, Librarian's Room.
l, Room to receive Effects of Smithson.
m, Mineralogical Cabinet

n, n, Central Corridor.
o, o, Cloisters.
p, Carriage Porch.
r, r, Main Northern Tower
s, Main Southern Tower.
t, Campanile.
u, Octagonal Tower.
v, v, Towers containing Elevators.
w, Bell Towers.
x, Apse.
y, Small Campanile.
z, Small Tower with private Stairway.

SECOND   FLOOR.

FIRST   FLOOR.

Scale of feet.

neer on active duty with the Corps of Engineers. The space was reconstructed in fireproof materials, using brick vaults and iron beams, as a grand, single hall 200 feet by 50 feet.

66. James Renwick, Jr., Floor Plan, detail of the first floor, wood engraving by J. H. Hall from *Hints on Public Architecture*, 1849.
Smithsonian Institution, neg. 92-15757.

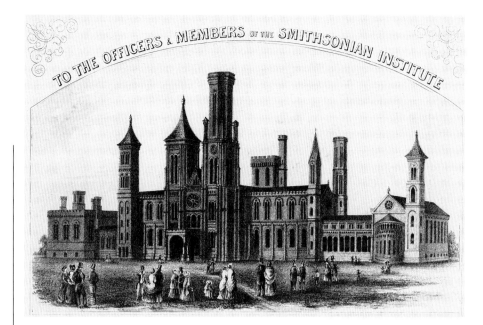

67. Cover sheet for the Smithsonian Polka, lithograph by A. Hoen & Co. from a drawing by Sindall, 1855. Smithsonian Institution Archives, Smithsonian Institution, neg. 82-3240.

Until 1855 the large first-floor hall remained unused. The Metropolitan Mechanics' Institute, established in 1852, requested permission to hold their 1855 fair in it. As president of the institute, Henry encouraged this use as a way of "favorably exhibiting the Smithsonian building to the public."[5] The exhibition, held on February 8, 1855, provided manufacturers, tradesmen, artisans, and inventors an opportunity to display their products.[6] In honor of this occasion, a polka & schottisch dedicated to the officers and members of the Mechanics' Institute was composed. A second polka, called the Smithsonian Polka, illustrated here, was composed in the same year. The sheet music covers for these pieces, likely written to commemorate the opening of the building, featured the image of the Smithsonian Building.[7]

68. Museum Hall, woodcut from William J. Rhees, *An Account of the Smithsonian Institution . . . ,* **ca. 1856.** Smithsonian Institution, neg. 43804-H.

Joseph Henry intended, upon the closing of the Metropolitan Mechanics' Institute exhibition, to erect three tiers of cases to run the length of the room,[8] but such an arrangement was never constructed. This engraving appears to have been executed before the hall was built because the artist depicted the room with a triple-tiered arrangement. Another aspect of artistic license was the appearance of gas sconces lining the long central corridor.

69. Henry M. Bannister and Henry W. Elliott with Henry Horan, the watchman, in the Lower Main Hall, looking west, photograph, ca. 1863–65. Private collection.

When the National Museum was established in the Lower Main Hall, exhibits were installed in cases down the center of the room as well as along the sides. Posing next to the large, circular meteorite, which came to the Institution in 1863, were Henry M. Bannister and Henry W. Elliott, who were Smithsonian employees as well as roommates in one of the highest North Tower rooms. Sporting a cap was Henry Horan, the watchman.[9]

In accepting the collections of the defunct National Institute, Joseph Henry insisted that the government assume the costs associated with the care and housing of the national collections. Consequently, cases were designed by a well-known government architect, Thomas Ustick Walter, the Architect of the Capitol.[10] These, along with cases transferred from the Patent Office, were filled with natural history specimens, many collected by officers of exploring and surveying expeditions such as the Wilkes Expedition of 1838–42. In addition to specimens of birds, mollusks, and other wildlife, the National Museum displayed exotic items such as "Egyptian and Peruvian mummies" and the so-called cannibal cooking pots from the "Feegee Islands." The museum exhibition was not restricted to preserved specimens; in one of the window cases were live snakes from New Jersey.[11]

70. Visitors to the museum, Lower Main Hall, looking east, photograph, 1867. Smithsonian Institution, neg. 60-144-A.

The visitors in this 1867 photograph posed in the center of a newly decorated Lower Main Hall. Although fire had ravaged the upper part of the building in 1865, the Lower Main Hall was relatively untouched as a result of the fireproof con-struction adopted after the collapse of 1850. Repairing water damage in the Lower Main Hall gave architect Adolf Cluss the opportunity to enhance the walls and ceiling with delicate stencil work.[12] Two large, portable stoves pro-vided additional heat to this cavernous space, because Renwick's original radiant wall hot-air system proved insufficient.[13] The collection of the National Museum rapidly expanded to fill all the space available in the hall, necessitating the construction of new glass cases. By late 1867, two tiers of cases had been erected across the east end.

■

The expansion of the museum into other areas of the Smithsonian Building allowed for the redistribution of specimens among the halls. The Lower Main Hall was de-voted to the natural history or zoological collections. Filling the center of the hall were casts of prehistoric mammals. The most dramatic was artist Benjamin Water-house Hawkins's cast of the Hadrosaurus, later considered an inaccurate recon-struction.[14] To serve as bases for the mas-sive plaster models of Hadrosaurus, Meg-atherium, and others, the old slant-top cases were modified.[15] Placing the casts on the cases resulted in an inventive use of the cavernous space and brought the objects closer to visitors on the balconies. These towering models remained in the hall until the mid-1880s, when they were moved to the National Museum Building.

**71. Hadrosaurus in the Lower
Main Hall, photograph, 1874–82.**

Private collection.

**72. Lower Main Hall, photograph,
ca. 1886.** Smithsonian Institution, neg.
NH-4494.

The completion in 1881 of the first National Museum Building (known today as the Arts and Industries Building) enabled Secretary Spencer Baird to rearrange the collections. The birds, shells, mollusks, and some fish remained as the primary exhibition in the Lower Main Hall. Mounted on the balcony railings were framed prints from John James Audubon's *The Birds of North America*, placed here as decorative scientific illustrations appropriate to the Smithsonian's collections. Crenellated cases from the balconies were placed in the center of the hall, allowing the balconies to be gradually given over to the curators of the divisions exhibiting in the space.

■

The change of the Lower Main Hall from solely an exhibition area to a combined research and exhibition space reflected the evolving field of museum theory. Articulated at the Smithsonian by Assistant Director of the National Museum George Brown Goode, this viewpoint saw the growth of the museum toward an organization combining the collection of objects for record and research with education that would be "the most comprehensive and instructive museum in the world." The museum of research, providing a comprehensive collection to curators and students, was located on the balcony spaces, while the educational museum was arranged in more accessible public space.[16]

In 1882 the curators of Fishes and Marine Invertebrates moved their offices for cataloging and arranging collection specimens to the north balcony [Fig. 73], and they were soon followed by the departments of Birds and Mollusks, which were transferred to the south balcony [Fig. 74]. Behind the photographer [Fig. 73], a spiral staircase in the northwest tower led down to the West Range, which had been recently arranged for the exhibition of fish, and continued into the basement, where additional, albeit undesirable, storage was available. Mary Jane Rathbun, assistant curator of Marine Invertebrates, wrote that in descending these stairs to the basement she "soon learned to make a loud noise at the door, else the rats would jump out upon [her]."[17]

73. Department of Marine Invertebrates on the north gallery of the Lower Main Hall, photograph, March 1904.

Smithsonian Institution, neg. 15879.

74. Department of Birds on the southeast gallery of the Lower Main Hall, photograph, ca. 1886.

Smithsonian Institution, neg. 6063.

75. Lower Main Hall with the initial Graphic Arts exhibits, looking west, photograph, ca. 1913. Smithsonian Institution, neg. 25450.

The arrangement of the Lower Main Hall was again affected in 1911 by the completion of another museum building (the National Museum of Natural History). With the natural history specimens removed to the new building, the Lower Main Hall was to be devoted to the uses of a library, with related exhibits.[18] The displays of Graphic Arts, moved to the Smithsonian Building in 1912, were considered appropriate to the library because they illustrated the processes for printing and binding books as well as those for producing prints.[19] During this transitional period, a few of the ornithological exhibits remained on display.[20] The Audubon prints, hung prominently from the balcony railings, provided a link in concept between the graphic works of art and the bird specimens, presaging the eventual transfer of these prints to the Division of Graphic Arts.

76. Lower Main Hall, looking east, after the demolition of the galleries, photograph, 1914. Smithsonian Institution, neg. 28051.

As the function of the Lower Main Hall changed completely to that of a library with related exhibits, the hall was accordingly reconstructed. The galleries, with the old exhibit cases on which they rested, were demolished to make way for new steel book stacks. For the first time since the exhibition of the Mechanics' Institute in 1855, if only briefly, the hall consisted of one open space. A large, hinged diamond-shaped pane had been installed in each of the windows at a time when openings were needed to provide ventilation for offices on the galleries. Some of the original iron railings from the galleries, shown leaning against the wall, were reused by the architectural firm of Hornblower & Marshall in the design of the book stacks.[21]

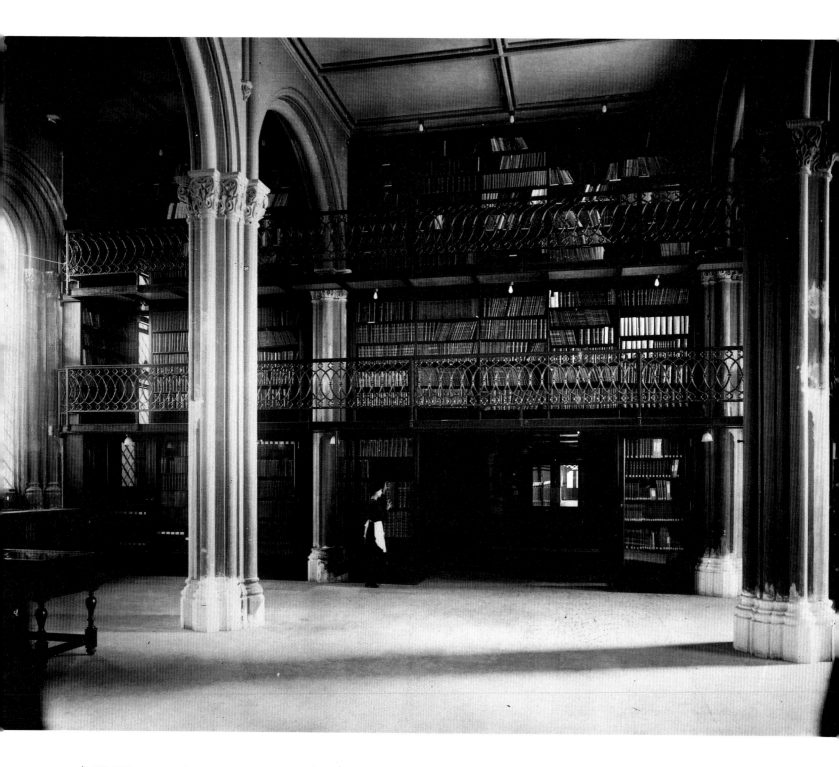

77. Library at the east end of the Lower Main Hall, photograph, 1914. Smithsonian Institution, neg. 60591.

The east end library shelves were finished and filled with books for this photograph, taken for display in the Smithsonian exhibit at the 1914 Panama-Pacific Exposition. From the patchy condition of the plaster and paint, it is clear that renovations were still ongoing. During the First World War, the Lower Main Hall became a lounge for soldiers, especially those drilling on the National Mall. Museum hours were extended, and in the Lower Main Hall "adequate facilities for letter writing were provided, and the room has been filled with soldiers daily during their rest periods."[22]

78. Graphic Arts exhibition in the Lower Main Hall, looking east, photograph, ca. 1920. Smithsonian Institution, neg. 22351.

During this rearrangement for library space, the central portion of the hall had been reserved for Graphic Arts exhibits, including both prints and photography.[23] In 1919 and 1920 watercolors of North American wildflowers painted by Mary Vaux Walcott, wife of Secretary Charles D. Walcott, were exhibited. These watercolors were later reproduced in a lithographic edition that faithfully captured the colors of the originals by means of a special four-color printing process on rag paper, later named "the Smithsonian Process."[24] Also visible in the low exhibit cases were the large photographs of Yellowstone National Park taken by Secretary Walcott.[25] The space was kept light and open through the use of these low cases, light-colored walls, and new light fixtures in a neoclassical style.[26]

79. Conference on the Future of the Smithsonian Institution, photograph, February 1927. Smithsonian Institution, neg. 17884-A.

The Graphic Arts exhibits were removed temporarily to make way for an important exhibition illustrating the range of Smithsonian activities and research. In February 1927 a special exhibition was set up in conjunction with the Conference on the Future of the Smithsonian Institution. A series of booths with tables and cases for exhibition of specimens, wall charts, and diagrams introduced the accomplishments of the Institution's various departments. Seated in front of an impressive twenty-three-foot-high column of books dramatizing the range and number of Smithsonian publications were many prominent citizens.[27] Left to right in the front row were Secretary of the Treasury Andrew Mellon, Secretary of State Frank Kellogg, President Calvin Coolidge, Chief Justice William H. Taft, and Smithsonian Acting Secretary Charles G. Abbot. Between Coolidge and Taft was Secretary of Commerce, later President, Herbert Hoover.

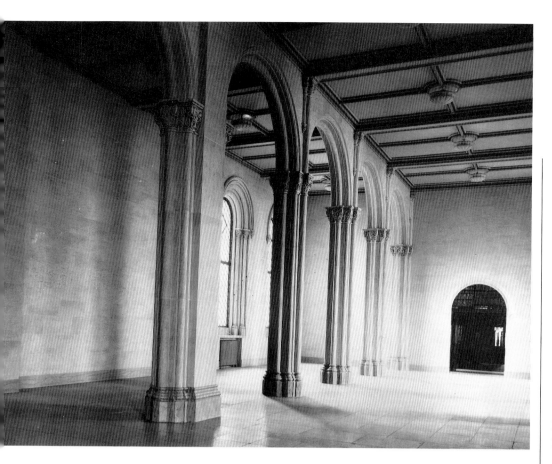

In this newly redecorated hall was installed the exhibition that the committee regarded as an "index," designed to inform visitors in a concise visual manner about all the Smithsonian's activities. Arranged as a series of alcoves, the "Index Exhibit" remained in the Lower Main Hall for over twenty years. Each of the eight alcoves contained a brief descrip-

81. "Index Exhibit" in the Lower Main Hall, looking west, photograph, 1941–42. Smithsonian Institution, neg. 34522-B.

80. Lower Main Hall under renovation, looking east, photograph, 1940. Smithsonian Institution, neg. 93-2427.

After removal of the temporary informational exhibition, the hall reverted to the display of Graphic Arts. Beginning in 1939, however, the idea for an exhibition presenting the Smithsonian as a whole was reintroduced. Secretary Abbot commented that, as a result of the Smithsonian's growth, visitors needed some guide to the Institution. Consequently, he appointed a committee to recommend plans for "a series of exhibits in the Smithsonian main hall that would portray in popular form the work of the Institution in many branches of science."[28]

The redecoration of the room reflected the modernist taste of the period. Walls were stripped and resurfaced with a hard plaster finish specially prepared to resemble both the texture and the color of a pale marble. At each end of the hall, new walls were erected to conceal the steel bookcases.[29] These walls, each constructed thirty feet into the Lower Main Hall, reduced its grand length by approximately one third but restored a sense of order by concealing the busy activity within the book stacks.

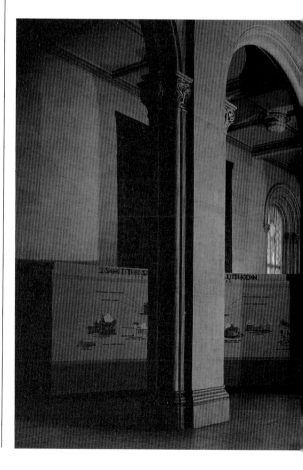

tion of a different department of the Smithsonian, simply illustrated with a model or diorama and other supporting exhibits. The departments of Astronomy, Geology, Biology, Radiation and Organisms, Physical Anthropology, Cultural Anthropology, Engineering and Industries, and Art were all represented. Another display addressed the history and founding of the Institution, its organizational structure, and the National Zoological Park. Only a few objects were shown, and the labels were kept as short as possible in an effort to streamline communication.[30]

In the 1950s Secretary Leonard Carmichael perceived opportunities for exhibiting in the hall the history of the Institution and its staff. While modernization of exhibits was the dominant theme of the decade, an appreciation of the historic character of the building was beginning to emerge. The modernized informational exhibition proposed for the Lower Main Hall would focus not on the branches of the Smithsonian, as had the "Index Exhibit," but on its people and history. The exhibition was to be clearly subordinated to the hall, which was to be renovated as "a semi-Gothic, baronial 'great hall.' "[31]

By 1959 planning had begun for the area that was now referred to as the "original Great Hall."[32] Although this plan was never put into effect, the designation "Great Hall," implying a gathering place, was adopted and established the character of this space.

82. "Index Exhibit" in the Lower Main Hall, looking west, photograph, 1941–42. Smithsonian Institution, neg. 34522.

83. 125th Anniversary of the Smithsonian Institution in the Great Hall, photograph, 1971.
Smithsonian Institution, neg. 72-4898.

Even before the arrival of a new Secretary, S. Dillon Ripley, the exhibition in the Great Hall had been viewed as an outdated and inadequate index of overall Smithsonian activity.[33] Planning began on renovation of the Great Hall in 1964, in preparation for the bicentennial of James Smithson's birth. While the Great Hall was still to be used as exhibition space, opened again to its original length of 200 feet, discussion ensued also on its use as "reception center, visitor center, and resting place" furnished in period pieces and providing information as well as respite.[34]

The decorative scheme was seen as creating an atmosphere appropriate to the building's history. The primary visual change was the use of strong colors, such as green, gold, and rust. The pillars were painted to resemble marble, a technique popular in the Victorian era, to "offer the only relief to an otherwise colorless room."[35] Carpet colors were chosen to harmonize with the overall scheme and support the restoration, giving the room a unity of color effect while covering the hard terrazzo floor of earlier decades.[36]

In 1971 a committee on the Great Hall planned to soften its stark appearance by adding furniture, such as the tufted and fringed velvet ottomans, and by hanging large paintings and architectural drawings.[37] The committee opposed the then current use of the hall for miscellaneous temporary exhibitions. They felt that the Great Hall should provide information on the events and exhibitions at the various Smithsonian museums, along with directions to them.[38] This idea evolved by 1971 into the mounting of the 125th Anniversary Exhibition in the Great Hall and South Tower, with each of the museums represented by a case of objects and a display.

84. Federal City exhibition in the Great Hall, 1976. Color slide in the Collection of the Office of Architectural History and Historic Preservation.

Education and visitor information were themes emphasized by the Bicentennial exhibition "Federal City: Plans and Realities," which filled the Great Hall from 1976, the year of the nation's two hundredth birthday, until its removal ten years later. By means of this exhibition, visitors to the Great Hall could both learn about the history of the planning of Washington, D.C., and locate themselves in relation to the museum buildings of the Smithsonian and the monuments of the capital. Highlights included the original models created for the Senate Park Plan (McMillan) Commission of 1901, depicting Washington at the turn of the century and the marble neoclassical city envisioned by the architects of the plan.

■

A 1983 decision to expand the Visitor Information and Associates' Reception Center solidified the designation of the Great Hall as the central location for information and public service.[39] Opened in 1987, the renovated hall featured a large, central information desk; numerous interactive video terminals; giant electronic wall maps, which guided visitors to other tourist sites in the city; and, by 1992, a gift shop. The east and west ends of the hall, which had been walled off in 1940 to create office space, were converted into movie theaters and rest rooms respectively. In the theaters an introductory film describing the activities of the entire Smithsonian ran continuously. The modern electronic techniques for transmitting information were expressed in the decor, which reflected a postmodernist reinterpretation of a Victorian setting. In this environment, with its palette of muted colors, the visitor became a participant in the information exchange. The intent of this renovation was to create, in the Great Hall, a doorway to the entire Smithsonian.

85. Visitor Information and Associates' Reception Center in the Great Hall, photograph by Richard Strauss, 1992. Smithsonian Institution, neg. 92-16586.

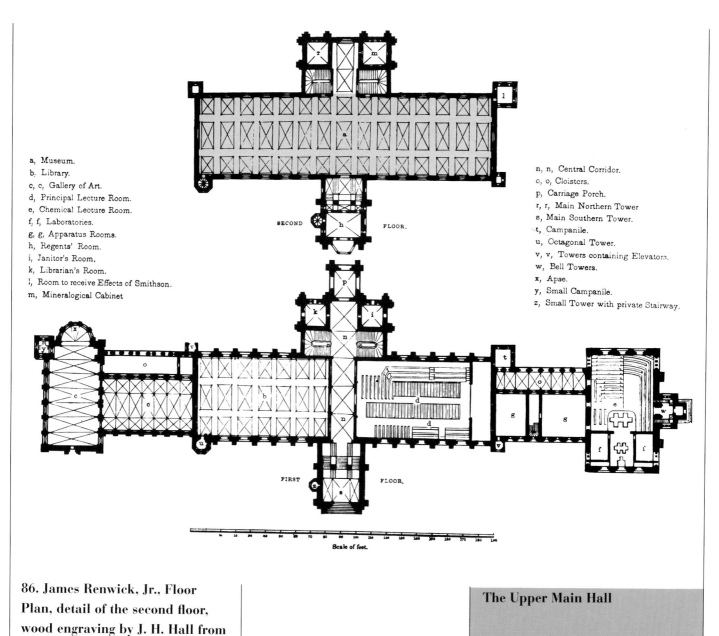

a, Museum.
b, Library.
c, c, Gallery of Art.
d, Principal Lecture Room.
e, Chemical Lecture Room.
f, f, Laboratories.
g, g, Apparatus Rooms.
h, Regents' Room.
i, Janitor's Room.
k, Librarian's Room.
l, Room to receive Effects of Smithson.
m, Mineralogical Cabinet

SECOND FLOOR.

n, n, Central Corridor.
o, o, Cloisters.
p, Carriage Porch.
r, r, Main Northern Tower
s, Main Southern Tower.
t, Campanile.
u, Octagonal Tower.
v, v, Towers containing Elevators.
w, Bell Towers.
x, Apse.
y, Small Campanile.
z, Small Tower with private Stairway.

FIRST FLOOR.

Scale of feet.

86. James Renwick, Jr., Floor Plan, detail of the second floor, wood engraving by J. H. Hall from *Hints on Public Architecture*, 1849.

Smithsonian Institution, neg. 92-15757.

The Upper Main Hall

Beginning with Robert Mills's first design in 1841, a vast and unobstructed museum hall on the uppermost floor was a desired characteristic of every plan for a Smithsonian building. Although the second floor was designated as a museum in the 1849 plan, when the building was completed in 1855, the second floor had been partitioned into three chambers, housing an enormous lecture hall, an apparatus room, and a gallery of art. Until the fire of 1865, which destroyed the entire second floor, these rooms played an important and active role in the Smithsonian's "diffusion of knowledge." Only after the building was reconstructed was the hall turned over to museum use. Filled with specimens illustrating the history of human activity in the Americas, the grand second-story hall flourished as a museum for over forty years.

The expansion of the Institution after the turn of the century cleared the Smithsonian Building's upper floor of exhibits. Assigned to the Department of Botany, the hall was gradually decked over and partitioned to provide space for offices and collection storage. When the completion of the Natural History Building's west wing in 1965 provided a new home for the Department of Botany, the last museum-related bureau left the Smithsonian Building. While the renovation that followed restored the great public spaces of the first floor, the Upper Main Hall was divided into two floors, providing numerous offices for a scholarly center. Only the library/meeting room for the scholars created at one end alluded to the grandeur of the original hall.

87. Museum Window, wood engraving by Bobbett & Edmonds from *Hints on Public Architecture*, 1849. Smithsonian Institution, neg. 92-15756.

The entire second floor of the main section of the building was designated as a large museum room in Robert Dale Owen's description in *Hints on Public Architecture* [Fig. 86]. Ample light, provided by the two-story-high windows, was a critical element. The "Museum Window" [Fig. 87], consisting of two pointed arches within a round-headed arch, similar to one reputed to have come from a building designed by Robert Dale Owen, suggested that Owen worked closely with James Renwick, Jr., on some elements of the design.[40] The long unobstructed space, free from columns or staircases, was central to the room's success as a museum.

When the building opened to the public in 1855, however, there was no museum running the length of the second floor. The space housed a large lecture hall, flanked on either side by smaller chambers containing an apparatus room and a gallery of art, intended to serve also as meeting places for associations. Together the arrangement of the second-floor rooms afforded "facilities for meetings of large associations which have for their object the promotion, diffusion, or application of knowledge."[41]

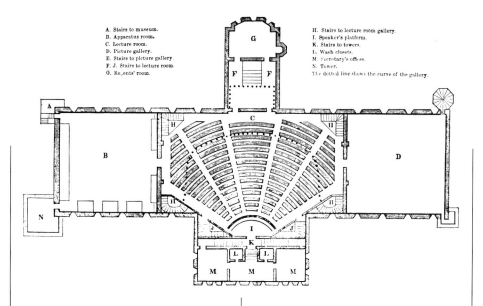

A. Stairs to museum.
B. Apparatus room.
C. Lecture room.
D. Picture gallery.
E. Stairs to picture gallery.
F. J. Stairs to lecture room.
G. Regents' room.

H. Stairs to lecture room gallery.
I. Speaker's platform.
K. Stairs to towers.
L. Wash closets.
M. Secretary's offices.
N. Tower.
The dotted line shows the curve of the gallery.

88. Floor Plan of the Upper Main Hall, woodcut from William J. Rhees, *An Account of the Smithsonian Institution . . . ,* **ca. 1856.** Smithsonian Institution, neg. 43804-S.

In the Smithsonian's *Annual Report for 1854,* Joseph Henry praised the new lecture hall, stating that "it is believed that this room is the most perfect of its kind in this country, and that it will serve as a model for apartments of a similar character."[42] He had worked very closely with Barton S. Alexander of the U.S. Corps of Engineers in the design of the hall.[43] Henry described this room as

somewhat fan-shaped, and the speaker is placed as it were in the mouth of an immense trumpet. The sound directly from his voice, and that from reflection immediately behind him, is thrown forward upon the audience.[44]

The placement of the lecture hall on the second floor of the building, instead of on the first as originally indicated in Owen's plan, provided a number of advantages. By orienting the hall in a north-south direction, Alexander and Henry were able to extend it into the towers, gaining an extra twelve feet.[45] An unobstructed width of one hundred feet, greater than that possible in any other area of the building, was also achieved.[46] Henry strove to create a hall in which every member of the audience not only would see the experiments performed but also would clearly hear the explanation of them.[47] To this end Henry, with Alexander Dallas Bache, conducted acoustical experiments in the primary halls and churches of Philadelphia, New York, and Boston; they also examined Montgomery Meigs's plan for the new chambers in the Capitol building extensions.[48] Learning from these examples, the Smithsonian designers were able to provide Washington with a particularly effective and quite large lecture and meeting hall.

∎

The success of the lecture hall led Henry to write that "the influence the Institution is having on the character and reputation of the city of Washington is by no means small. The free lectures . . . tend to promote the intelligence and morality of the citizens."[49] The room, with its gallery, could hold over 1,500 people, nearly double the capacity of the earlier East Wing lecture room.[50] Although Henry voiced concern that the lectures might reach only a local audience, which he felt was inappropriate for a national institution, he took comfort in the dissemination of these lectures through Smithsonian publications. He also advocated the lectures as a way to interest important academics in the Institution's work.[51]

The lecture series was often difficult to attend in poor weather, because of the muddy paths of the National Mall. To ease access, Henry advocated laying boards on the path across the grounds to the Tenth Street bridge over Tiber Creek. This canal, which stretched from the Potomac River to the foot of Capitol Hill, further isolated the building from downtown Washington. As late as 1868, Henry reported to the Board of Regents that visitors to the Institution were

shocked and their olfactory nerves outraged, in approaching the building from the city, by having to cross that most disgusting object known as the "canal," though for years it has done no service of any value in that capacity. It is, in fact, a Stygian pool, from which are constantly ascending in bubbles, as from a caldron, mephitic vapors. That part of it

89. Lecture Hall in the Upper Main Hall, woodcut from William J. Rhees, *An Account of the Smithsonian Institution . . . ,* ca. 1856. Smithsonian Institution, neg. 43804-K.

which bounds the Smithsonian grounds and those of the Agricultural Department, on the north, consists of a basin 150 feet wide, extending from Seventh street to Fourteenth street. Into this is poured most of the excrementitious matter of the city, which is suffered to decompose into offensive gases, and exposes with each ebb of the tide a mass of the most offensive matter conceivable.[52]

90. Apparatus Room in the Upper Main Hall, woodcut from William J. Rhees, *An Account of the Smithsonian Institution . . . ,* ca. 1856. Smithsonian Institution, neg. 43804-G.

To the east of the lecture hall was the apparatus room, containing a significant collection of scientific instruments, most of which had been donated by Dr. Robert Hare of Philadelphia. Hare had accumulated much of the apparatus during his twenty-nine years as professor of chemistry at the University of Pennsylvania Medical School. In the illustration, Hare's electrical machine is visible on a platform on the left side of the room. The room was arranged to allow for a popular science experiment demonstrating the effect of static electricity.[53] The hair of a person sitting in the thronelike chair on the platform under the machine would be made to stand on end as a result of an electric charge.

**91. Gallery of Art in the Upper
Main Hall, woodcut from William
J. Rhees,** *An Account of the
Smithsonian Institution . . . ,*
ca. 1856. Smithsonian Institution,
neg. 43804-D.

The room to the west of the lecture hall was arranged as a gallery of art. It was opened with a series of portraits of prominent North American Indians deposited by the artist, John Mix Stanley, in the hope of convincing the government to purchase the extensive collection.[54] In 1858, over one hundred Indian portraits painted by Charles Bird King were added to the room [Fig. 92]. Also displayed in this gallery was a copy of "one of the most celebrated statues of antiquity," known as the "Dying Gladiator."[55] The location of this sculpture, far removed from the statues exhibited in the West Range, made a conscious visual comparison between the plight of the Native American peoples and the dying heroes of a classical world. The juxtaposition encompassed the sentiment that the destruction of Native American communities and life-styles was considered inevitable and as tragic as the loss of the ancient world.[56]

Henry articulated the role of the gallery as he saw it, that

it is a sacred duty which this country owes to the civilized world to collect everything relative to the history, the manners and customs, the physical peculiarities, and, in short, all that may tend to illustrate the character and history of the original inhabitants of North America.[57]

92. Charles Bird King portraits in the Gallery of Art, Upper Main Hall, photograph, 1858. National Anthropological Archives, Lot 80-47, Smithsonian Institution, neg. 78-12052.

The fire of 1865, in which the central roof collapsed, began over the picture gallery. Workmen, rearranging the gallery on an unusually cold January day, inserted a stovepipe into the brick lining of the building rather than into a flue; smoke and embers collected for a number of days in the space under the roof, and the resulting fire was burning fiercely before it was discovered.[58] The fire utterly destroyed the second floor of the building but left unscathed the Lower Main Hall, with its natural history specimens. The wings, one of which housed the Smithsonian library, were also undamaged. Even though the destruction was much less extensive than it could have been, the fear of fire would spur extensive reconstruction of the building's interior throughout the next half century.

93. Illustration of the fire of 1865, woodcut from a sketch by Philip Wharton in *Harper's Weekly*, 1865.
Smithsonian Institution, neg. 58765.

Although this popular illustration showed the entire building engulfed in flames, the fire was in fact confined to the second floor and the upper levels of the towers. When the fire was discovered, Secretary Henry was in his office in the North Tower preparing the *Annual Report for 1864*. He described "a singular noise above our heads and after listening a few moments I exclaimed 'the house is on fire!' . . . I soon learned that the whole extent of the under side of the roof of the main building was one sheet of flame."[59]

During the brief period before the roof began to fall into the building, efforts were made to save the more important holdings, but only seven paintings of Stanley's extensive collection were rescued.[60] William DeBeust, in charge of maintenance for the building and the apparatus, recounted that he

commenced pulling down the pictures on the south side. . . . I had a large pile ready to be carried out, but [other Smithsonian workers] did not come back, being probably frightened. About six feet square of ceiling had fallen down, exposing the fire. . . . I still remained until another part of the ceiling fell down, no one coming to assist. I slid two of the pictures down the ladder and took them into . . . [the] basement.[61]

94. Smithsonian Building after the fire of 1865, photograph by G. D. Wakeley, ca. 1865–67.
Smithsonian Institution Archives, Smithsonian Institution, neg. 30792-A.

The most immediate concern after the fire was replacement of the main roof, to protect the exhibits in the Lower Main Hall. A temporary roof was erected within three days.[62] It remained until the spring of 1867, when it was replaced with an iron and slate roof designed by Adolf Cluss.[63] Cluss, a Washington architect born and trained in Germany, came to the Smithsonian "warmly recommended" by the Mayor of the District of Columbia for his work designing local school buildings.[64] He remained the primary architect for the Institution until 1890. In this role he was responsible for reconstructing nearly the entire interior of the building in fireproof materials, to ensure that no such loss would occur again. The fire of 1865 thus had a significant impact on the appearance of the building's interior spaces.

In the reconstruction of the interior, Henry decided not to return the Upper Main Hall to use as a lecture room. During the Civil War, more and more people had petitioned to use the lecture hall to promote their political interests.[65] Not wanting to spend Smithson fund monies on the museum, Henry allowed the second floor to remain unfinished for nearly six years. He suggested that the government either purchase the building and assume responsibility for running the National Museum or increase the funds for supporting the collections.[66] In 1870 Congress responded by appropriating $20,000 for expansion of the museum under the Smithsonian's management.[67] This appropriation enabled the Institution to begin preparing the large second floor for museum use.

Reconstructing the second floor as one large, open museum realized for the first time Robert Dale Owen's original plan for this space. For nearly forty years the hall flourished as one of the principal galleries for the National Museum collections. Henry praised the room as exhibition space, noting the absence of columns such as those in the Lower Main Hall.[68] Successive reorganization of the exhibits during the second half of the nineteenth century reflected the changing attitudes toward museum display and the evolution of study in ethnology and anthropology.

Henry sought a design for the new museum from Benjamin Waterhouse Hawkins, an English artist who had made his reputation as a modeler of casts of prehistoric mammals.[69] Hawkins's finished drawings featured galleries, which would have provided additional exhibition space at the expense of the unobstructed space that Henry so valued. The room was to be enhanced by portrait medallions of American Indians and paintings of their daily life.[70] This decorative embellishment advanced Henry's supposition that for "museums to be effective as means of adult education [they] must be attractive and the articles of purely scientific interest put away in drawers for special exhibition."[71]

95. B. Waterhouse Hawkins, Ethnological and Paleozoic Museum, plan, April 1871.
Smithsonian Institution Archives, Smithsonian Institution, neg. 91-10552.

96. B. Waterhouse Hawkins, Internal arrangements of Ethnological and Paleozoic Museum, rendering, April 1871.
Smithsonian Institution Archives, color transparency in the Office of Architectural History and Historic Preservation.

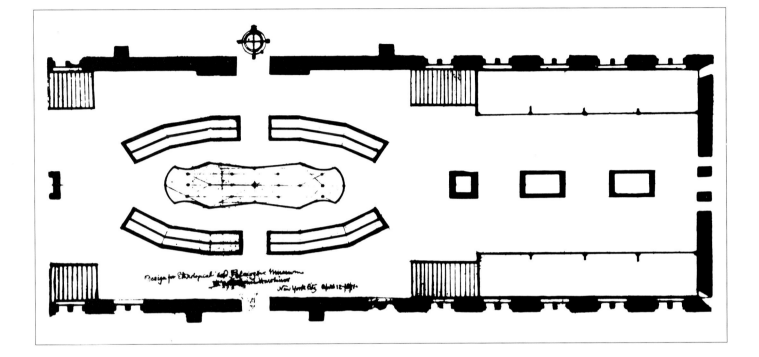

97. Megatherium in the Upper Main Hall, photograph, 1872.
Private collection.

Hawkins's plan for the museum was never carried out; the appropriation allowed only a simple reconstruction of the room.[72] The vast hall was opened with a varied collection of mammals and casts of prehistoric creatures, as well as an ethnological display. In the center of the room stood a Megatherium model made by Henry Ward, the owner of Ward's Natural Science Establishment in Rochester, New York. For an additional sum the Smithsonian received from Ward the decorative bronze railing with miniature prehistoric mammals.[73]

The most striking architectural features of the room were the elaborate door surrounds. These portals with round-headed arches were surmounted by battlements recalling the exterior of the building. Each contained a tympanum of circular glass mullions. Adolf Cluss, who supervised the renovation of the room, was most likely responsible for these grand doorways.[74]

The enormous scale of the room tended to dwarf even the mammoth specimens on display, making the hall appear barren and stark. Soon the space would be more successfully used by filling the room with cases for the vast collections of ethnological specimens.[75] Scarcely a year later, in 1872, Henry initiated a reordering of the hall for ethnology, believing that to be the more significant and current scientific study.[76] North American Indian life was prominently featured in the sketches by George Catlin.[77] To accommodate the eth-nological specimens, distinctive cases were designed by Henry Ward and built by local craftsmen. Elaborately veneered with walnut and bird's-eye maple, the cases had large panes of English plate glass and were designed to be dustproof. Henry, while praising the cases' imposing effect, warned that they would be "out of place in the large room. . . . What is wanted in this case is architectural effect not minute filigree work."[78]

98. Cases being assembled among the specimens in the Upper Main Hall, photograph, 1873. Private collection.

100. Museum in the Upper Main Hall, looking east, photograph, ca. 1885–90. Smithsonian Institution, neg. 21346.

99. Museum in the Upper Main Hall with Tsimshian housefront, looking west, photograph, ca. 1879–85. Smithsonian Institution, neg. 2962.

The hall, arranged with the ethnological and archeological collections, no longer overwhelmed the specimens. The variety, height, and number of cases, combined with the artful arrangement of specimens, contributed to the cohesion of the architecture and the exhibition. Spears and bows and arrows from various tribes, decoratively grouped in patterns on the walls, made an effective transition from the tops of the cases to the coffered ceiling. In like fashion, the placement of the busts on top of the cases contributed to the successful ordering of the lofty space. An immense painted housefront, acquired from the Northwest Coastal Indians for display at the Philadelphia Centennial of 1876, provided a focal point on the west wall.[79] The principle that guided the arrangement of the hall brought objects of like material and function together, emphasizing their similarities regardless of when or by whom they had been manufactured.[80] A similar philosophy supported the exhibition at the Blackmore Museum in Salisbury, England, with which the Smithsonian exchanged both information and specimens. By focusing on one time period, the Blackmore collections demonstrated "that the workings of human minds and human hands in the stone age have produced very similar results in every quarter of the globe."[81]

A strikingly different aesthetic of exhibition design, more serious and scholarly in tone, governed the arrangements by the mid-1880s. With the erection of the National Museum Building in 1880–81, George Brown Goode, newly appointed Assistant Director of the National Museum, initiated a redistribution of the collections. The ethnological collections were transferred to the new building, enabling expansion of the exhibition of archeological specimens. Items that had enhanced the earlier arrangements, such as the spears and busts, were removed.[82] Only materials that appeared to be directly supportive of the primary exhibition, such as the Aztec calendar stone, remained on the walls.

cated objects within a cultural context, identifying geographical region and historical period.[83] Using the following analogy, Wilson explained the shifting philosophical intent: "In historic museums we study the object displayed; in the prehistoric museum we rather study the man who made the object, and therefore the necessity of having all his relics and remains assembled together."[84] The entire western end of the rearranged hall was given over to the models of pueblos, along with their inhabitants' objects of daily and ceremonial life. As part of the new system, "synoptical cases" were placed at the entrance to the museum room to provide a general overview of the entire exhibition. The cases were billed as the first instance of a distinction between those visitors with a few minutes to browse and those who came for education and scientific study.[85]

In 1891 the museum underwent a complete reorganization of the collection display. Thomas Wilson, Curator of Prehistoric Anthropology, urged that the outdated system of classification be replaced. In its stead he proposed a scheme that lo-

101. Zuni model in the southwest corner of the museum in the Upper Main Hall, woodcut from *Frank Leslie's Monthly,* **February 1890.** Smithsonian Institution Archives, Smithsonian Institution, neg. 92-16512.

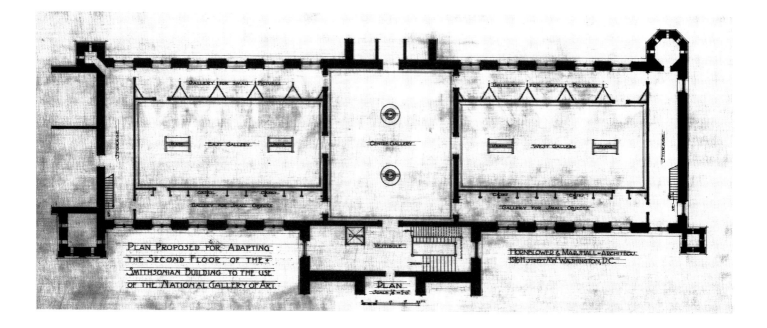

Anticipating the removal of the museum collections to the new building under construction in 1907, the Smithsonian proposed to dedicate the second floor to a national gallery of art. Valuable bequests received by the Institution during 1906 and 1907—such as Charles Freer's extensive Asian art collection, Harriet Lane Johnston's collection including English portrait paintings, and William T. Evans's collections of American works—considerably advanced the status of the Smithsonian's art holdings.[86] While the archeological collections were still in place, designs were drawn up for a noble suite of rooms to house fine art.

102. Hornblower & Marshall, Proposed National Gallery of Art in the Upper Main Hall, plan, 1907. Smithsonian Institution Archives, Smithsonian Institution, neg. 89-14395.

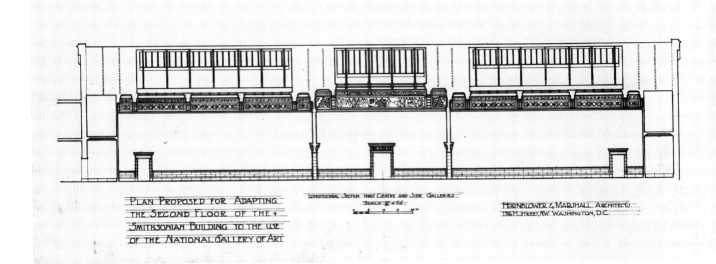

**103. Hornblower & Marshall,
Proposed National Gallery of Art
in the Upper Main Hall, drawing,
1907.** Smithsonian Institution Archives,
Smithsonian Institution, neg. 89-14397.

The proposal for the Gallery of Art would have transformed the second floor into a suite of three rooms, echoing the 1855 arrangement of this space. The impressive galleries, designed by Hornblower & Marshall, resembled in their Beaux Arts monumentality this architectural firm's designs for the new museum building across the National Mall. A central gallery, with skylights providing natural light, was framed by rooms on the east and west and long, narrow galleries for sculpture or small pictures along the north and south [Fig. 102]. The galleries were elegantly decorated with classical detail, including allegorical friezes over the main entrances [Fig. 103]. These plans were never realized because the appropriation for a national gallery of art was denied.[87]

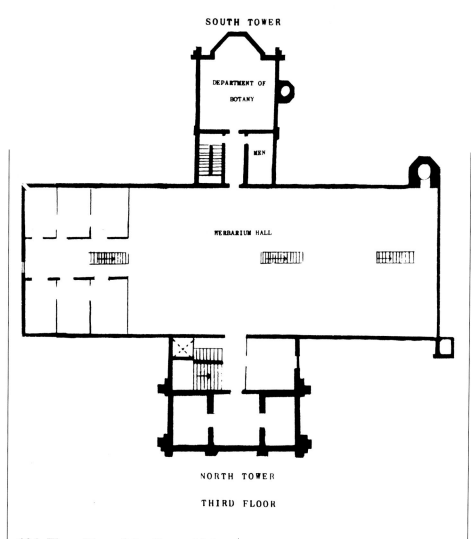

SOUTH TOWER

DEPARTMENT OF
BOTANY

MEN

HERBARIUM HALL

NORTH TOWER

THIRD FLOOR

104. Floor Plan of the Upper Main Hall, ca. 1959. Smithsonian Institution Archives, Smithsonian Institution, neg. 77-10934.

The second floor was vacated in 1910, when the collections moved to the nearly completed National Museum Building (now the National Museum of Natural History). Rather than return the space to public use, Smithsonian administrators decided to turn the hall over to the Herbarium, a collection of dried plant specimens mounted and systematically arranged for reference.[88] The commitment of this floor to a research-oriented purpose resulted in the destruction of the hall's architectural integrity. A large deck was built at the east end and enclosed to provide two floors of office and laboratory space. Additional space for the storage of specimens, which were so numerous that they could hardly be kept in sequence, was made available by construction of a steel deck or mezzanine over the west end

105. Department of Botany in the Upper Main Hall, looking west, photograph, ca. 1965. Smithsonian Institution, neg. 92-16558.

of the hall in 1928.[89] This deck was expanded in 1954 to cover the rest of the hall, essentially creating two floors out of the Upper Main Hall.[90] Three metal staircases connected the two levels [Fig. 104]. With no further room for expansion, the cases had been stacked three high on the upper level by the time the Herbarium moved out of the Smithsonian Building in 1965. This once grand space thus became a warehouse for the Division of Plants.

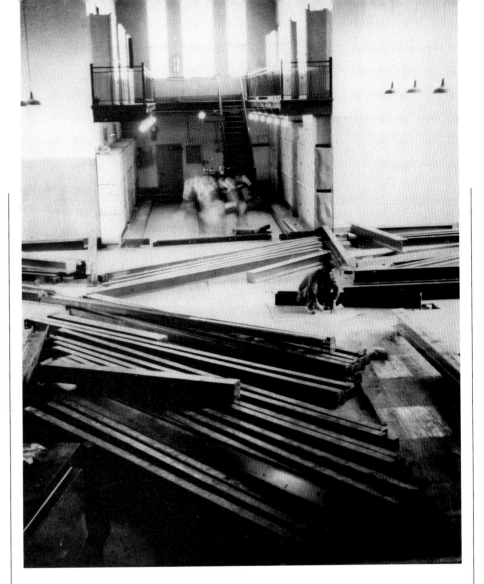

106. Removal of the Department of Botany from the Upper Main Hall, photograph, 1965. Smithsonian Institution, neg. 74-946.

In 1965 the entire Herbarium collection was transferred to the newly erected west wing of the Natural History Building. The cases were removed through one of the windows to a temporary elevator erected on the exterior.[91] The move was carefully programmed to retain the order of the cases, because the specimens were stored sequentially. The steel frame deck was then dismantled in preparation for a full renovation of the second-floor area.

During the period preceding the renovation, the empty hall was engaged for a creative arts program called Summer Adventures for Youth.[92] The cavernous second-floor hall was again decked over in 1968, providing two floors of offices to house a center for scholars. Although the Smithsonian Center for Advanced Studies was never created, its place in the building became the Woodrow Wilson International Center for Scholars. Announcing its arrival, a *Washington Post* editorial stated that

the whimsical Norman castle on the Mall seems to us a most appropriate place to get the center off to a good start. . . . the dignified informality and humble flamboyance of its recently renovated rooms and halls ought to inspire just the right atmosphere for scholarly creativity.[93]

107. Octagonal rotunda of the Upper Main Hall in use as the reception area for the Woodrow Wilson International Center for Scholars, photograph, 1972.
Smithsonian Institution, neg. 72-9363.

This "dignified informality" was well illustrated in the layout of the new floors in the Upper Main Hall. In a conscious rejection of a typical standardized office grid, the architects, Chatelain, Gauger and Nolan, were instructed to avoid "a central corridor and even rectilinear pattern. . . . An unbalanced or irregular corridor plan is desired with varying size room arrangements."[94] At the center of this new arrangement was an octagonal reception room, which served as the hub for the scholars' daily activities. Although the historic character of the Upper Main Hall had been largely eliminated in the renovation, the spirit of the building was evoked with nineteenth-century furnishings.

108. West end of the Upper Main Hall in use as the library for the Woodrow Wilson International Center for Scholars, photograph, 1972. Smithsonian Institution, neg. 72-4900.

One area of the original museum hall was preserved during the renovation.[95] The room thus created was designated for use as a meeting room and has served also as the Wilson Center Library. Only here could be seen the full "Museum Window" [Fig. 87] and the circular rose window illustrated in *Hints on Public Architecture.* The rose window, bricked up after the fire of 1865, was uncovered for the first time, admitting the light of the western sun. Together these windows expressed on the interior the building's medieval revival style.

109. Octagonal rotunda of the Upper Main Hall in use as the reception area for the Woodrow Wilson International Center for Scholars, photograph by Richard Strauss, 1992. Smithsonian Institution, neg. 92-16571.

After twenty years, the octagonal reception area was enlivened with a new period decorative scheme reflecting the influence of the Aesthetic movement in the United States in the last quarter of the nineteenth century. This movement, an "artistic" taste in the decorative arts, was made popular by the Philadelphia Centennial Exposition of 1876. There American artists and designers were exposed to art objects from many nations and cultures, especially Japanese, Turkish, and Moorish. The absorption of exotic influences in American culture exemplified by the Aesthetic movement has provided an interesting atmosphere for the dialogues of scholars from around the world.

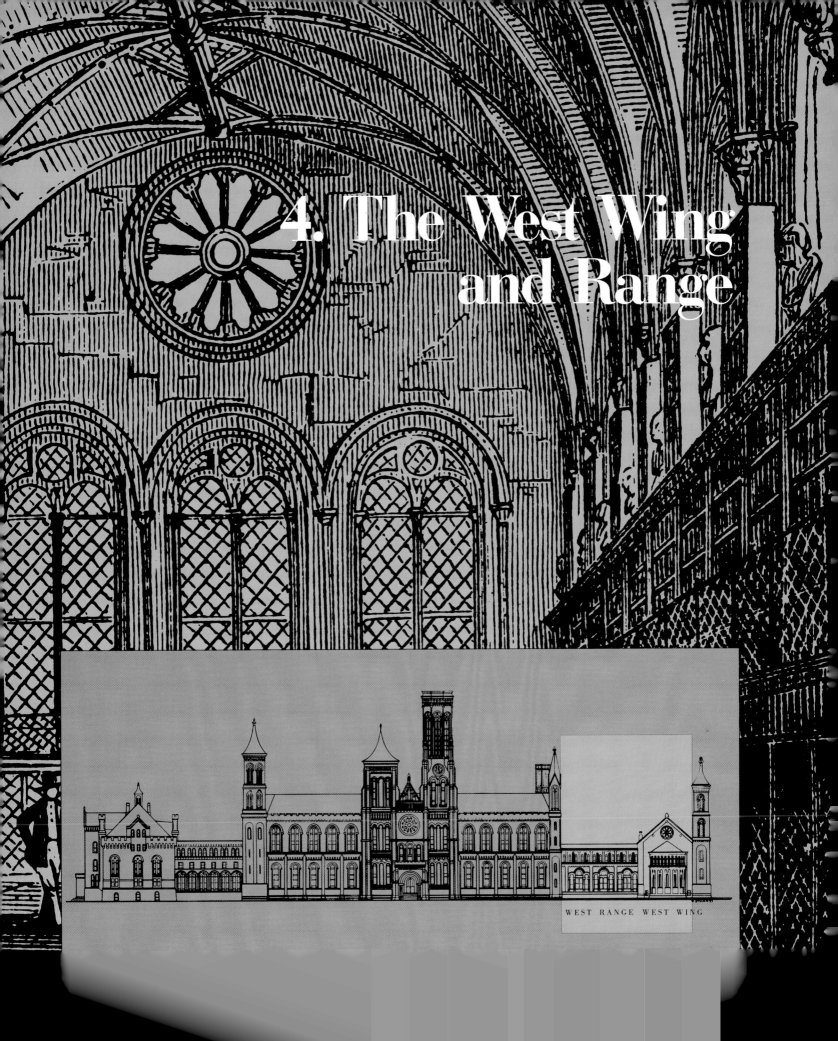

4. The West Wing and Range

WEST RANGE WEST WING

*T*he west end of the building, with its soaring single-story halls and abundant natural light, was designed with the Institution's public functions in mind. The teaching college that Robert Dale Owen envisioned for the Smithsonian would have required many lecture halls. As designed by architect James Renwick, Jr., this grand, well-lit space was planned for such a use, with its rounded apse providing an admirable lecturer's podium. The high windows and skylights, which made the West Wing a successful design for a lecture hall, were also considered ideal for a gallery of art. Although the entire west end was designated as an art gallery in the 1849 plan, when it was completed the West Wing served as the Smithsonian's library, and the West Range was adapted for use as a reading room. It was not until after the fire of 1865, when the Institution's library collections were transferred to the Library of Congress, that the West Wing and Range were wholly dedicated to use as exhibition space.

Beginning with the displays of Mineralogy and concluding with those of Graphic Arts, the West Wing and Range provided educational exhibitions for over one hundred years. The renovation of the Smithsonian Building in the late 1960s, combined with the completion of the Museum of History and Technology in 1964, represented a dramatic change for this area. The last museum exhibits remaining in the building were removed, and the grand Gothic spaces of the west end were restored as communal gathering places. The dedication of this area to a lounge and dining room signaled the new status of the building as a visitors' center.

In the 1849 floor plan for the Smithsonian Building, both the West Wing and the West Range were destined to hold a gallery of art. Although the West Wing with its rounded apse derived its form from ecclesiastical models, it was never intended to function as a chapel. Rather it was meant to form a visual contrast with the blocky form of the massive East Wing. Robert Dale Owen explained this striking dissimilarity by stating that the west end, "intended to contain a Gallery of Art, intimates, by its lighter proportions and airier forms, the spirit, more of grace and ornament, of its destination."[1] By 1848, however, when the exterior of the West Wing and Range was completed, plans were in progress to house in it the growing library collection instead.

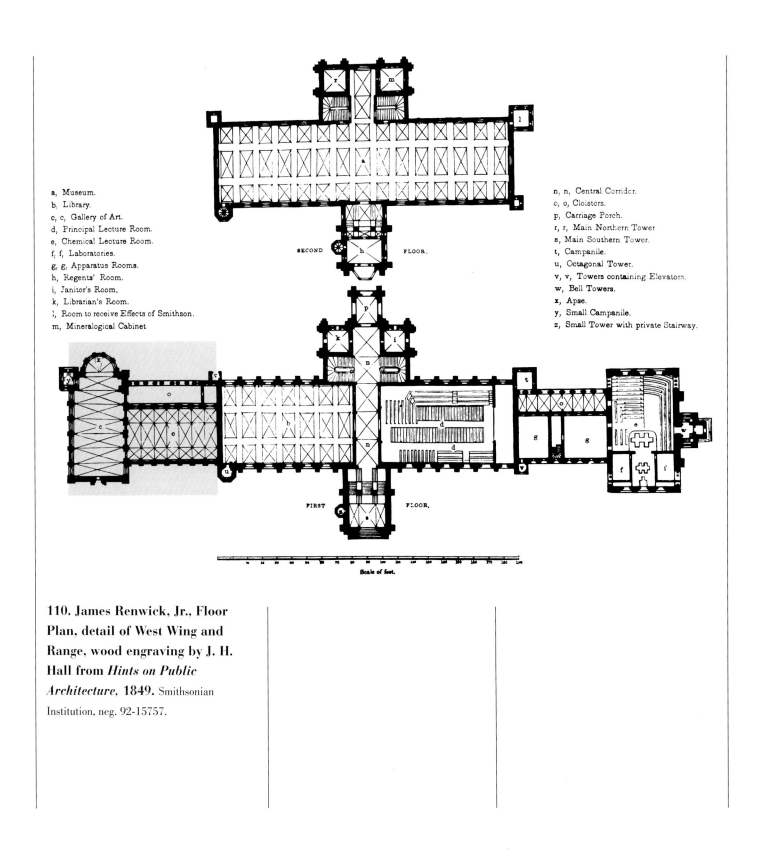

a, Museum.
b, Library.
c, c, Gallery of Art.
d, Principal Lecture Room.
e, Chemical Lecture Room.
f, f, Laboratories.
g, g, Apparatus Rooms.
h, Regents' Room.
i, Janitor's Room.
k, Librarian's Room.
l, Room to receive Effects of Smithson.
m, Mineralogical Cabinet

n, n, Central Corridor.
o, o, Cloisters.
p, Carriage Porch.
r, r, Main Northern Tower
s, Main Southern Tower.
t, Campanile.
u, Octagonal Tower.
v, v, Towers containing Elevators.
w, Bell Towers.
x, Apse.
y, Small Campanile.
z, Small Tower with private Stairway.

SECOND   FLOOR.

FIRST   FLOOR.

Scale of feet.

110. James Renwick, Jr., Floor Plan, detail of West Wing and Range, wood engraving by J. H. Hall from *Hints on Public Architecture*, 1849. Smithsonian Institution, neg. 92-15757.

111. Library in the West Wing, ca. 1852–54. Smithsonian Institution, neg. 60739. The authors have made every effort to locate the original image, without success.

In preparation for the library books, which were installed in March 1850, the perimeter of the room was furnished with tall wooden cases. Prints, acquired from George Perkins Marsh, an early Regent and Representative to Congress from Vermont, were treated not as works of art but as illustrations of the history of engraving. Representing another aspect of printing, they were displayed in the West Wing with the books of the library. High above the floor hung scenes of Indian life and portraits painted by John Mix Stanley.[2] This unusual placement had been necessitated by the lack of wall space in the building, which was still under construction when the paintings arrived in 1852.

THE SMITHSONIAN, LIBRARY ROOM.

112. Reading Room in the West Range, woodcut from William J. Rhees, *An Account of the Smithsonian Institution . . . ,* **ca. 1856.** Smithsonian Institution, neg. 78-3854.

Concurrent with the use of the West Wing as a library, the connecting Range was designated as a public reading room. The leading periodicals and scientific journals published in the United States, Great Britain, and parts of Europe were readily available to visitors of all ages. Fourteen-year-old Francis Ormand French wrote in his diary of 1851,

Today I went to the Smithsonian Institution where for some hours I read, having an excelent [*sic*] time for a good book is truly a companion and I know of nothing which is more entertaining. I hope to repeat this visit frequently.[3]

The high vaulted ceiling above a clerestory, and the rows of columns with their clusters of delicate colonnettes, made a strong statement in the Gothic style, leading many who worked in the building to call this room the Gothic Hall.[4]

113. Library in the West Wing, woodcut from William J. Rhees, *An Account of the Smithsonian Institution . . . ,* **ca. 1856.** Smithsonian Institution, neg. 43804-L.

The West Wing was rearranged in 1857 to provide two stories of alcoves for bookcases, as the number of books in the library continued to increase. This second level, approached by a staircase in the small West Tower, more than doubled the space available.[5] Busts arranged along the top of the second tier represented prominent men of arts and letters as well as science, such as Thomas Jefferson, Daniel Webster, John Milton, and Robert Fulton. The incorporation of busts of admirable worthies into the contemplative mood of a library was characteristic of the mid–nineteenth century.[6]

114. Sculpture on the south side of the West Range, photograph, ca. 1865. Smithsonian Institution Archives, neg. SA 18-A.

Additional busts arrived with the collections of the National Institute, precipitating the transformation of the West Range from a reading room into a gallery of art.[7] Along the south side of the hall stood a cast of a famous classical model, known as the "Venus de Medici," visible behind a decorative iron railing [Fig. 114]. Of the busts on the north side of the hall [Fig. 115], Martin Van Buren, eighth President

of the United States, is recognizable as the third from the front. Joel Poinsett, founder of the National Institute and the man for whom the poinsettia plant was named, was captured in the portrait bust on the far side of the Sleeping Child, both executed by sculptor Ferdinand Pettrich. The collection thus mixed aesthetically valuable objects with those valued for their historical associations.

115. Sculpture on the north side of the West Range, photograph, ca. 1865. Smithsonian Institution Archives, Smithsonian Institution, neg. SA 18-B.

The replacement of the reading room with a sculpture gallery marked the beginning of the metamorphosis of the West Wing and Range into museum halls. These rooms remained assigned to the National Museum for the next one hundred years. The Smithsonian's library collections were permanently transferred to the Library of Congress in 1866, along with the Marsh Collection of prints.[8] While the West Range was converted to ethnological exhibits, the West Wing, closed to the public, was used to store natural history specimens preserved in alcohol and duplicate specimens for distribution.[9] Some measures were taken to fireproof the dormant West Wing,[10] and the hall was redecorated, with the walls scored and painted to resemble the exterior building stone.

116. Meeting of the National Academy of Sciences in the West Wing, photograph, April 1871.
Smithsonian Institution, neg. 10844.

The first event held in the newly refurbished West Wing and adjoining West Range was the April 18, 1871, meeting of the National Academy of Sciences, over which Joseph Henry presided.[11] Created to provide to the nation the benefits of science and the scientific method, the Academy was intended to have the prestige and permanence of a national organization without becoming an instrument of Congress. After its founding in 1863, it was housed in the Smithsonian Building for over fifty years, until its present building, designed by Bertram Goodhue, was dedicated in 1924.[12] Mary Henry, the Secretary's oldest daughter, was present for this photograph; she is visible on the far right.

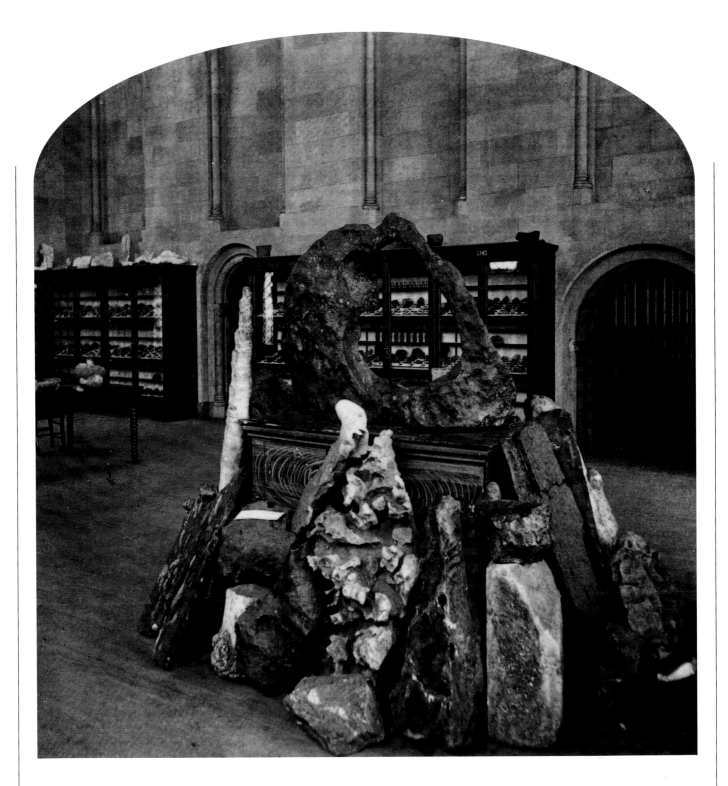

117. Mineralogical specimens on display in the West Wing, photograph, ca. 1871. Private collection.

Following the meeting of the National Academy of Sciences, the hall was opened with an exhibition of mineralogical specimens. A giant meteorite on display in the center of the room had been brought to the Smithsonian in 1863 from an area south of Tucson, Arizona. Described as resembling "an immense signet ring," it was then considered among the largest known. Before 1871 the meteorite had been displayed in the Lower Main Hall [Fig. 69].[13]

To secure the West Wing for collections, the floor was made fireproof in April 1871 by replacing its wooden support with shallow brick vaulting on iron beams. During the renovation of the wing, the floor was raised to create enough space in the basement for laboratories,[14] which were used for preserving in alcohol the fish, reptiles, and invertebrates that constituted the National Museum's natural history collections. According to its inscription, this woodblock illustration was made from sketches and photographs by Henry W. Elliott, a naturalist, artist, and employee of the Smithsonian.

**120. The West Range, looking east
toward the Lower Main Hall,
photograph, ca. 1871.** Private
collection.

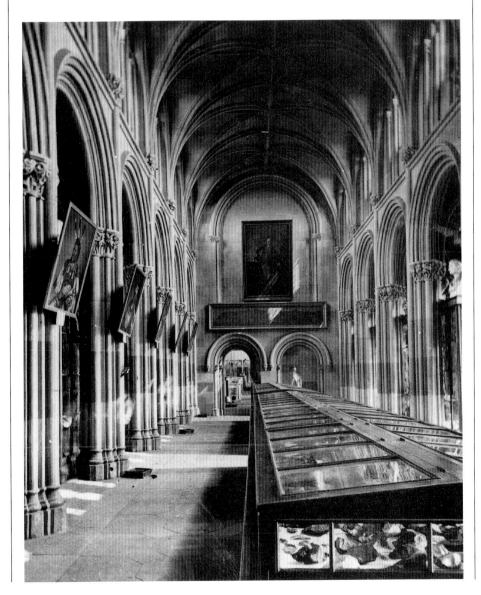

Vestiges of the earlier gallery of art remained in the newly created ethnological
hall in the form of two oil paintings and
several marble and plaster busts on the
tops of the exhibit cases. The portrait of
the French historian and statesman Fran-
çois Pierre Guillaume Guizot, painted in
1841 by the American artist George Peter
Alexander Healy, hung at the west end of
the hall [Fig. 119]. Directly opposite,
above the entrance to the Lower Main
Hall, hung one of the full-length portraits
depicting George Washington after the
Battle of Trenton, painted by Charles
Willson Peale [Fig. 120]. The juxtaposition was particularly fitting, because Guizot, an authority on republican government, took special interest in the
founding father.[15]

As Congress had allocated no money
for the development of a museum in the
large Upper Main Hall, the West Range
was furnished in 1868 with cases to display ethnological specimens of North
American Indian workmanship. Artifacts
from other cultures, such as China, Japan,
and prehistoric France, were also exhibited in the room for purposes of comparison.[16] Along the arcades hung portraits
depicting Indian delegates visiting Washington between 1858 and 1869, painted
by Antonio Zeno Shindler, an artist employed by the National Museum.[17]

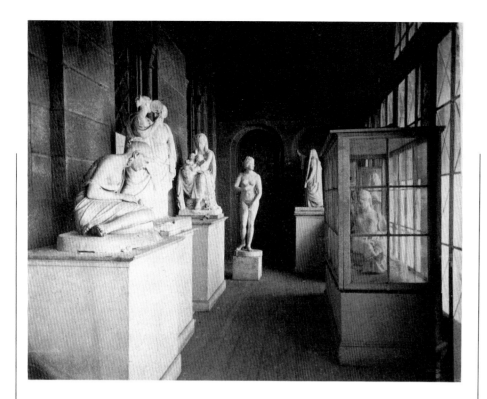

121. Cloister, north side of the West Range, photograph, ca. 1871–72. Smithsonian Institution, neg. 82-3279.

When the West Range was given over to ethnological displays, the sculptures that had been on exhibition there were moved to the cloister along the north facade.[18] On both the east and west of the north facade ran open, arcaded walkways, small-scale copies of late medieval cloisters. The cloistered walkway was a vestige of the early design, when Robert Dale Owen had striven to make the Institution a free public college. Proving drafty and ill-suited to the actual purposes of the Institution, the cloisters had been enclosed with windows within a few years of the building's completion.[19]

■

122. Model of a Japanese warrior in the cloister, photograph by C. Seaver, Jr., ca. 1873. Private collection.

The west cloister was chosen in 1871 for a photography studio because of its row of large windows, which provided even, diffused northern light. Before the studio was established here, the Institution's photography had been carried out by the light of the large bay window in the Regents' Room. This wax figure dressed in the armor of a Japanese warrior was one of many specimens brought into this room to be photographed. Thomas W. Smillie was the Smithsonian's first official photographer, appointed in June 1871. Smillie also became the first custodian of the Section of Photography, created in 1896, the precursor of today's Division of Photographic History. Smillie's studio occupied this cloister room until 1875, when it was moved to a small building erected in the south yard expressly for the use of the photographer and the taxidermists preparing exhibits for the Centennial Exposition in Philadelphia.[20]

At the conclusion of the 1876 Centennial Exposition, a great many of the specimens and exhibits were donated to the National Museum and exhibited in the West Wing. From France came a pair of mammoth Haviland pieces entitled *The Struggle* and *Prosperity*. The two eight-foot-high terra-cotta covered jars commemorated the American struggle for independence in 1776 and the celebration of the prosperity and industry of the American people at the exposition. A more directly symbolic tribute was the sculptural group *America*, on loan from Henry Doulton & Co. of England. A full-size terra-cotta reproduction of one of the marble corner pieces from the Albert Memorial in London's Hyde Park, this colossal group held a prominent position in the center of the hall.[21]

123. The group *America* in the West Wing, photograph, ca. 1879.
Private collection.

124. The West Range redecorated, photograph, ca. 1882. Smithsonian Institution, neg. 2601.

The enormous terra-cotta group *America*, still on loan when this photograph was taken, around 1882, was visible through the arched door leading from the West Range to the West Wing. The West Range was redecorated in 1882, when it was prepared to exhibit fish. The numerous glass jars containing specimens preserved in alcohol were placed on view in narrow cases running from the decorative piers to the wall.[22] Architectural elements were picked out in rich colors, creating a kaleidoscopic decorative scheme. A patterned floral motif was stenciled within each of the three shallow arches over the entrance to the wing. A second stylized floral stencil decorated the area over the arches. Henry Horan, the building superintendent, commented that its new appearance added "a freshness and beauty to that Hall which it could never boast of before."[23]

125. Cluss & Schulze, section of the West Range, blueprint of fireproofing scheme, March 1887. Smithsonian Institution Archives, Smithsonian Institution, neg. 2533-C.

By the late 1880s, most of the building had been dramatically altered in the course of renovation to make it secure against fire. At this time only the West Wing and Range remained in an unfireproofed condition. In 1887 Congress appropriated $15,000 for fireproofing the West Range, which housed collections of specimens preserved in highly volatile alcohol.

The fireproofing of this space, with its decorative Gothic design, presented a particular challenge to Adolf Cluss and his partner, Paul Schulze. Its delicate architectural detail, clusters of colonnettes, and groin-vaulted ceiling proved impossible to duplicate in fireproof materials within the budget allotted. Although the architects attempted to preserve "the Romanesque general character of the building,"[24] the great expense and difficulty of

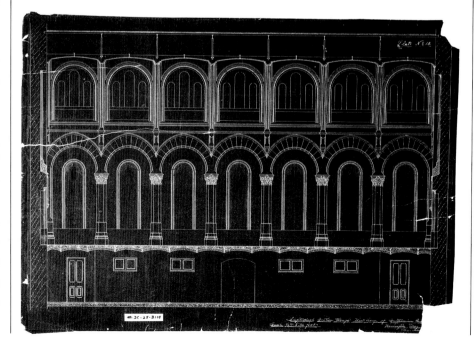

the work necessitated a simplification of the original design. The room after the fireproofing was markedly different from Renwick's "Gothic Hall." Short, massive columns replaced the original ones with their slender colonnettes, and the spidery groin vaulting of the ceiling was reduced to simple barrel vaulting. To enhance this stark composition, Cluss & Schulze proposed an elaborate decorative scheme.

126. Cluss & Schulze, section of the West Range, decorative scheme never adopted, May 1888.
Smithsonian Institution Archives, Smithsonian Institution, neg. 2531-H.

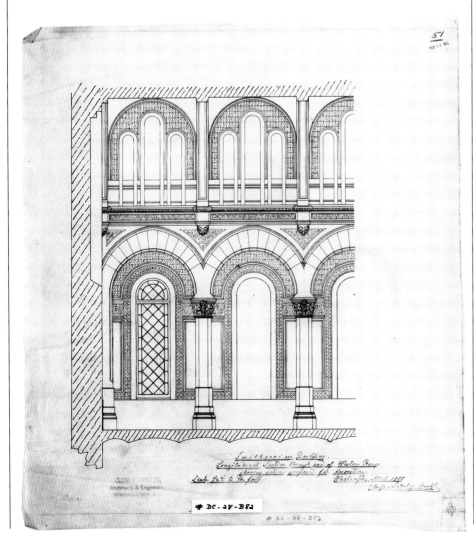

To soften and unify what must have seemed a severe, angular space in contrast to the former elegant interior, Cluss & Schulze prepared a set of black-and-white drawings illustrating a proposed decorative scheme. In an accompanying letter to the Secretary suggesting a color scheme, a vivid portrait of the room emerged:

The piers separating the naves with the surmounting arches to be treated in gray, as stone architecture, with the capitels [sic] of the piers in light marble tint with gilding of prominent parts. The side walls to have a base of maroon and to be done in a tasty green-gray tint with ornaments kept more brilliant but raised from the same tint. The window framings to be in warmer and more brilliant tints, as implied by the Romanesque style. The panels of the ceiling to be in a pale bluish tint with brilliantly decorated warmer moldings, etc.[25]

This decorative scheme, which was Cluss & Schulze's last project for the Smithsonian, was never carried out. A few years later, Edward Clark, the Architect of the Capitol, was chosen to supervise the fireproofing of the West Wing. Adolf Cluss provided a transition to this work by sharing his extensive knowledge of the building.

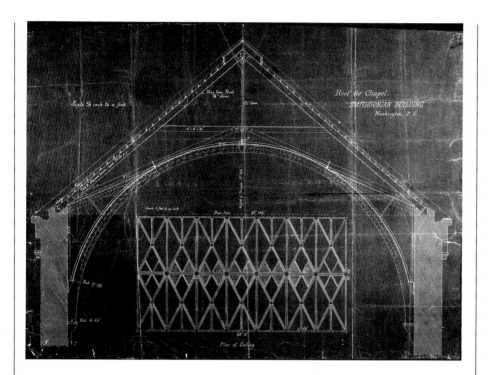

127. Roof for Chapel and Plan of Ceiling for the West Wing, fireproofing scheme, 1891.
Smithsonian Institution Archives, Smithsonian Institution, neg. 89-6888.

For the fireproofing of the West Wing, Cluss explained in a letter to Clark the importance of reproducing as closely as possible the ceiling and arches, despite the great cost:

in this room Prof. Henry made during 10 years all manner of experiments, to kill an intolerable echo, caused by the groined arch ceiling of wooden framework. Mr. [George Brown] Goode's judgment [is] that this obstinate ceiling is one of the chief beauties of the building, and must be perpetuated in fireproof materials.[26]

Congress appropriated funding in August 1890 for the fireproofing of the West Wing, stipulating that the work was to be carried out under Clark's supervision.[27] The two-year project involved replacing the wooden trusses with iron.

128. Marine invertebrates on display in the West Wing, photograph, ca. 1901. Smithsonian Institution, neg. 17381.

The West Wing reopened in early 1893 with a refurbished exhibition of marine invertebrates.[28] Huge plaster casts of an octopus and a giant squid, designed for the Tennessee Exposition of 1897, were later suspended from the ceiling.[29] Painted plaster casts such as these were considered by the head curator of the Department of Biology to be art objects rather than natural history specimens. Two compelling reasons for such representations in museum exhibitions were, first, the difficulty of preserving in alcohol such large specimens, and, second, the impossibility of retaining these creatures' real-life colors. For large specimens, no solutions to these problems were found suitable, except reproduction by model.[30]

129. Insects on display in the West Range, photograph, ca. 1902.
Smithsonian Institution, neg. 16849.

The display of insects also presented many challenges to curators at the turn of the century. The West Range had been turned over to the Department of Insects in 1897–98, although a cast from the Department of Fishes remained inexplicably in its place over the door to the Lower Main Hall. Great difficulty was encountered in providing a clean background on which to pin the insects that would not warp during changes in weather. Toward the end of 1901, a solution was found that used specially prepared cork and blotting paper.[31] The collection included nearly 1,500,000 specimens, but only about 2,700 of these, representing the most unusual species, were put on exhibition. In a break from past National Museum exhibits, descriptive labels were written in language the nonscientist could readily understand.[32] The thoughtful techniques devised by the staff of the Departments of Insects and Fishes to preserve and display specimens were indicative of the professional level to which the National Museum had risen at the beginning of the twentieth century.

A major reorganization of the National Museum collections was occasioned by the completion in 1911 of the new National Museum Building across the National Mall. Most of the exhibits in the Smithsonian Building were removed to the new museum, today known as the National Museum of Natural History. This transfer enabled the Division of Graphic Arts in 1912 to occupy all three exhibition halls on the Smithsonian Building's first floor—the West Wing, the West Range, and the Lower Main Hall. The Graphic Arts exhibits were left partially unfinished from 1914 to 1916, when all three halls were closed to the public because of extensive renovations in the Lower Main Hall.[33]

The closing of the West Wing in 1914 during the renovation allowed the hall to be used as a workroom for restoration of the "Star Spangled Banner," the garrison flag that flew over Fort McHenry in Baltimore, Maryland, during the War of 1812. This flag was immortalized in a poem written in 1814 by Francis Scott Key, which proved popular when subsequently set to music. At the time of this restoration, the song had not officially become the country's national anthem; it was so designated by an act of Congress in 1931. Originally measuring thirty by forty-two feet, the flag had been shortened by eight feet before its arrival at the Smithsonian; the missing parts, it was presumed, were cut up for souvenirs.[34] To preserve the flag, a team of seamstresses used a series of interlocking open buttonhole stitches to secure the tattered fragments to a backing of unbleached linen. One could imagine that the work took on a new meaning in the presence of the monumental statue of George Washington seated in the apse at the other end of the hall [Fig. 131].

130. Women repairing the "Star Spangled Banner" in the West Wing, photograph, 1914. Smithsonian Institution, neg. 27897.

131. Graphic Arts exhibits in the West Wing, with sculpture of George Washington in the apse, photograph, ca. 1925. Smithsonian Institution, neg. 23758.

Presiding over the hall was the neoclassical statue of George Washington executed by Horatio Greenough in 1841. It was transferred from the east lawn of the Capitol, where it had stood since 1843, after two years in the rotunda of the Capitol.[35] The Smithsonian placed the statue in the apse of the West Wing in 1908, in anticipation of the formal establishment of the National Gallery of Art; the "Chapel" was viewed as suitable for a hall of sculpture.[36] Because the legislation providing for a national gallery failed to pass through Congress, the hall had been turned over to the Division of Graphic Arts. The statue nonetheless remained there until 1962, when it was moved to the Museum of History and Technology (now

the National Museum of American History), which was under construction.[37]

The displays of Graphic Arts were neatly arrayed at the foot of the Greenough statue. Sylvester Koehler, the first Curator of Graphic Arts, had been largely responsible for both the initial growth of the collection and the direction of its development. He believed that the collection should "represent art as an industry," meaning that it was to illustrate all aspects of the printing process, aesthetic as well as technical.[38]

The cluttered appearance of the West Range in this photograph resulted from the transfer of a third of the exhibits from the Lower Main Hall when that space was transformed in 1940 into the "Index Exhibit." To improve the West Range exhibition, the Graphic Arts curators decided in 1938 to replace the museum cases dating from the late 1880s with modern, "good-looking" cases.[39] Visible on the fourth column from the left is one of many signs posted through the Institution directing visitors and staff to air-raid shelters. After the attack on Pearl Harbor, preparations began in earnest to protect the collections from anticipated raids. Collections in vulnerable tower rooms were moved to safer basement storage. Heavy objects suspended from ceilings or girders were taken down, and many specimens were boxed and crated.[40]

132. Graphic Arts exhibits in the West Range, photograph, ca. 1950. Smithsonian Institution, neg. 42618-A.

133. Printmaking studio of the Graphic Arts Department in the cloister, Robert Mooney in the foreground with Curator Ruel Tolman, photograph, ca. 1933. Smithsonian Institution, neg. 9794-B.

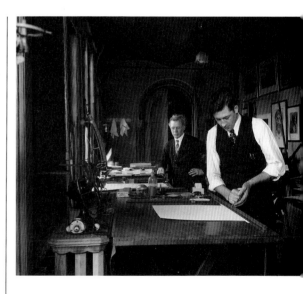

As a complement to the exhibits depicting the processes of the graphic arts, the division maintained a working printmaking studio in the cloister that had once been occupied by the photographer Thomas Smillie. The room reflected the architectural changes made in the 1887 fire-proofing of the West Range. By lowering the ceiling, Cluss & Schulze were able to insert a mezzanine story into the cloister, providing additional office space on the floor above this one.[41]

134. Newly renovated Graphic Arts exhibition in the West Wing, with Curator Jacob Kainen in the foreground, ca. 1960. Smithsonian Institution, neg. 43950-E.

In 1955, as part of Secretary Carmichael's Institution-wide plan of exhibit modernization, over 250 specimens from the Graphic Arts' West Wing and Range exhibitions were placed in storage. Jacob Kainen, Curator of the Division of Graphic Arts, stated in his report for the year that he

began a complete revision of the exhibits in the portion of the Smithsonian Building known as the "chapel" with a view to presenting a graphic explanation of the techniques of picture printing and to tracing the development of the important processes employed to reproduce pictures mechanically.[42]

Electric lighting was installed in the room for the first time, and by 1956 a portion of the new Graphic Arts exhibits was completed and opened to the public.[43]

135. Newly renovated Graphic Arts exhibition in the West Range, photograph, July 1958. Smithsonian Institution, neg. 92-15739.

The exhibits in the West Range, completed a few years after those in the West Wing, focused on the hand processes of etching, engraving, lithography, and silk screen. Fine prints by Dürer, Rembrandt, Delacroix, and Matisse were used as illustrations for these techniques.[44] These modernized Graphic Arts exhibits remained in the West Wing and Range until 1963, when they were transferred to the newly completed Museum of History and Technology (today known as the National Museum of American History) on the National Mall.

137. The Commons in the West Wing, photograph by Richard Strauss, 1992. Smithsonian Institution, neg. 92-16581.

To heighten the Gothic effect of the room, shields representing the coats of arms of famous men of letters and science from England, Scotland, Ireland, and Wales were mounted in 1971. Exhibited in the British Pavilion at the 1939 World's Fair held in New York, these shields were left in the United States upon the outbreak of World War II and eventually given to the Smithsonian. The coats of arms of Horace Walpole, William Penn, William Pitt, William Shakespeare, Sir Francis Drake, Edmund Burke, William Laud, Benjamin Disraeli, Sir Isaac Newton, Robert Blake, Geoffrey Chaucer, and Charles Darwin were displayed.[48]

The West Wing and Range, emptied of exhibits, were included in the programmatic development of a center for advanced studies to be housed in the Smithsonian Building. The planning committee determined that the west end should be reserved for use as a social center by the scholars.[45] The committee designated the West Wing as a dining room, or commons, and the connecting range as a lounge. Special attention was to be given to the design of the West Wing and Range.[46] The medieval character of these spaces and their stylistic associations with places of higher learning made them ideally suited to this new use.

136. The Commons in the West Wing, photograph, 1976. Smithsonian Institution, neg. 76-4139.

The West Wing was converted to a dining hall, named the Commons, a term suggesting the traditional dining rooms in historic English colleges. The room was painted in muted tones of tan, beige, and terra-cotta. Dominating the pale colors of the walls was the painted ceiling, consisting of gold stars on a deep blue background. This treatment was patterned after the Gothic chapel of the French kings, Sainte-Chappelle in Paris.[47] By the time the newly decorated West Wing was finished, it was to serve Smithsonian staff and guests, visiting scholars of the Woodrow Wilson International Center, and Contributing Members. Of the numerous vaulted ceilings in the original building, only the West Wing retained its evocative Gothic character.

138. The West Range, looking east, photograph, ca. 1972. Smithsonian Institution, neg. 72-4896.

In the renovation of 1970, the West Range became an extension of the dining facilities. A focal point of the room was a massive Gothic-style midnineteenth-century organ, made by William Davis of New York. Secretary Ripley, commenting on the first performance, given September 26, 1971, the night of the 125th anniversary of the Institution, stated that he hoped "it can be used often, including both planned recitals and impromptu practicing. Occasional five finger excercises [sic] at lunch time would be most uplifting to the spirit of the Commons."[49]

139. Associates' Reception Area in the West Range, photograph by Richard Strauss, 1992. Smithsonian Institution, neg. 92-16588.

At the beginning of 1975, anticipating an increased volume in visitors because of the upcoming Bicentennial, the Visitor Information and Associates' Reception Center suggested the use of the West Range as a lounge for members of the Smithsonian National Associates.[50] Chairs and sofas in which to relax during a long day at the museums were made available; by the windows large partner's desks provided places for writing postcards and letters. The midnineteenth-century furnishings selected were from the building's collection. The room, no longer considered an adjunct of the Commons dining hall, has since been partitioned to provide a quiet area for visitors.

5. The Towers

CAMPANILE

NORTH TOWER

FLAG TOWER

NORTHWEST TOWER

WEST TOWER

SOUTH TOWER (REAR OF BUILDING)

*J*oseph Henry, distressed at the prospect of James Smithson's gift being consumed by the erection of a large and ornate edifice, endeavored to have the Smithsonian Building completed with fewer towers.[1] Viewing the towers as the epitome of architectural excess, Henry stated that "the buttresses, turrets, and towers, while they add very little to the accommodation of the building, greatly increased the cost."[2] Nonetheless, the towers proved important in establishing the building's visual identity, as one nineteenth-century observer noted:

making nine in all, the effect of which is very beautiful, and which once caused a wit to remark that it seemed to him as if a "collection of church steeples had gotten lost, and were consulting together as to the best means of getting home to their respective churches."[3]

Beyond presenting a stylish impression, the towers were critical to the building's role as cradle of the Smithsonian's growth. Within the South Tower the Regents, the presiding body of the Institution, met regularly. The establishment of a crypt for benefactor James Smithson on the first floor of the North Tower symbolized a dedication to the Institution's history and Smithson's founding premise of "the increase and diffusion of knowledge." The first-floor room of the South Tower was selected by Samuel Langley for his Children's Room, a venture expressing outreach to new audiences. New ideas and governing principles have spread throughout the Institution from these tower rooms.

Staircases were placed within towers to maintain clear, open spaces in the main hall. At opposing corners of the Main Building rose small towers designed for freight elevators to haul heavy objects to the museum. The towers have also provided office space for many of the Institution's scholars, curators, and scientists. For a handful of men in the nineteenth century, some of the tower rooms furnished living quarters as well. The towers continue to provide offices for many Smithsonian employees, but only owls have been offered the opportunity to live in any of the Smithsonian's turrets in the last hundred years.

The South Tower

140. James Renwick, Jr., the South Tower, wood engraving by Bobbett & Edmonds, from Robert Dale Owen, *Hints on Public Architecture*, 1849. Smithsonian Institution, neg. 2534-E.

Rising solidly in the center of the south facade, the massive South Tower was the only part of the building truly reminiscent of a real castle. Embattlements along the roof and the small octagonal tower, mounting like a lookout, recalled fortified architecture. Divided into three parts, the exterior of the tower gave clues to the interior configuration. The room on the first floor, intended by James Renwick, Jr., as a vestibule, also served as part of the museum. Above this entrance was the Regents' Room. The uppermost room was used by Secretary Henry as an office.[4] These three stately rooms were differentiated on the exterior by the presence of the grand entrance door on the first, the protruding oriel window on the second, and a soaring double-arch window on the third. Until the fire of 1865, the union of interior use and exterior appearance remained unchanged.

141. South Tower, looking west, photograph, ca. 1860. Smithsonian Institution, neg. 87-8163.

142. South Tower, looking west, photograph, 1904–5. Smithsonian Institution, neg. 15681.

The South Tower was extensively damaged in the fire of 1865. Although it proved necessary to rebuild entirely the upper thirty feet, an effort was made to maintain as much as possible the original exterior appearance.[5] Once rebuilt, the tower did look much the same. However, the logic that Renwick had intended in distinguishing three grand floors was lost, because six floors now existed in the same space. To light these newly created rooms, Adolf Cluss inserted small circular windows [Fig. 142]. The form and size of these windows were chosen carefully to provide adequate light to workroom and storage areas without markedly altering the exterior architectural effect.[6] All the decorative features of the exterior were retained, including the niche originally intended by Renwick for sculpture. In 1980 it was finally filled with a late nineteenth-century neomedieval work, which seemed appropriate to the building; a figure of Saint Dunstan, which had graced the front of Westminster Abbey in London, was presented to the Smithsonian as a gift.[7]

Unlike the exterior, the interior spaces of the South Tower were altered considerably in response to programmatic changes under different Secretaries and in the course of repair of damage caused by the fire of 1865. The changes resulting from the fire were the most dramatic, reducing the original stature of the rooms by nearly half in some cases to provide new storage and office space. Alterations resulting from programmatic initiatives were primarily decorative.

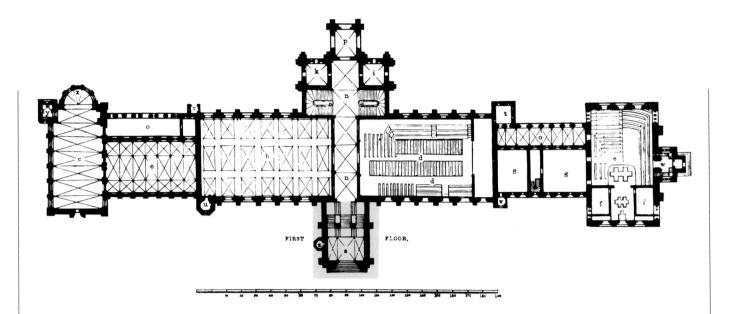

THE SOUTH TOWER ROOM

The first floor or South Tower Room was originally an extension of the building's main exhibition hall [Fig. 143]. According to the 1865 guidebook, a broad mix of objects was exhibited in this room, including a plank from a California redwood tree, an enormous piece of copper from a mine near Lake Superior, artifacts from Nicaragua, and a live alligator from Georgia.[8] One of the more prominent items was a marble sarcophagus erroneously thought to have held the remains of a Roman emperor [Fig. 144]. This sarcophagus had been brought to the United States from Syria in 1839 by Jesse Duncan Elliott, Commodore-in-Chief of the U.S. Navy in the Mediterranean, and presented as a final resting place for Andrew Jackson. The former President, however, declined the gift, on "the ground of repugnance to connecting his name and fame in any way with imperial associations."[9]

143. South Tower Room, detail of the Floor Plan, wood engraving by J. H. Hall, from Robert Dale Owen, *Hints on Public Architecture*, 1849. Smithsonian Institution, neg. 92-15757.

144. Syrian sarcophagus in the South Tower Room, photograph by F. H. Bell, 1867. Courtesy of the Kiplinger Washington Collection.

145. The Children's Room in the South Tower Room, color lithograph from the *Annual Report for 1901*. Color slide in the Collection of the Office of Architectural History and Historic Preservation.

Convinced that museums could provide a special environment conducive to learning in children as well as adults, Secretary Langley converted the South Tower Room in 1901 to a gallery of natural history exhibits for children. Langley felt that if they were to benefit from the educational possibilities in museums, a different approach to exhibit design would be necessary. In directives to his staff, he explained the design decisions from the point of view of the room's young visitors. Latin labels, commonly found in all natural history museum displays of the day, were to be replaced with poetic inscriptions; as Langley explained, identifying himself with children in trying to make suitable choices for the room,

we are not very much interested in the Latin names, and do not want to have our entertainment spoiled by its being made a lesson.[10]

Hornblower & Marshall designed the setting, from structure to furnishings.[11] On a massive table of craftsmanlike design in the center of the room sat a large aquarium filled with colorful fish.[12] Live specimens on view in the room were meant to encourage the child to marvel at nature's beauty. Under Hornblower & Marshall's influence, a shiny mosaic floor of red, blue, green, yellow, black, and white tiles was laid. New cases were made close to a child's height, placing the specimens within easy view. Constructed of light maple, these cases easily harmonized with the bright interior.[13] The number of specimens in these cases was reduced, too, so children would not be overwhelmed. The leafy wrought-iron gates, also designed by the architects, alluded to the natural world on the other side of the glass doors, making the doors less a barrier than a transition.

This theme of exploring the natural world, embodied in the exhibition itself, was also carried out in the room's decorative scheme. For the artistic design, Grace Lincoln Temple, an early twentieth-century designer who enjoyed great success in the interior decoration of federal public buildings, was chosen.[14] To create a bright, cheery environment, Temple selected luminous shades of green to cover the greater portion of the walls, which were sectioned off by gilded moldings. The green and gold of the walls were used also on the ceiling, where they were enriched by intense blues and rich browns.[15] Temple created a unique stencil for the wall frieze, a graceful parade of stylized birds in bright colors, which encircled the room. Inspired by the Celtic pages in Owen Jones's influential pattern book *The Grammar of Ornament*, Temple introduced a design reform aesthetic.[16]

146. Grace Lincoln Temple with the ceiling stencils for the Children's Room, photograph, ca. 1901. Smithsonian Institution, neg. 79-13846.

147. Ceiling of the Children's Room being painted, with Grace Lincoln Temple watching from the scaffolding, photograph, ca. 1900.
Smithsonian Institution, neg. 85-7821.

A similar decorative use of natural forms was found in the designs for the ceiling decoration. Langley had requested the recreation of a ceiling fresco by Correggio that he had seen in Parma, Italy, in which playful cherubs peered down at the viewer through a leafy arbor.[17] When an exact copy of this work proved prohibitively expensive, Temple was asked to develop a new decorative scheme. Her design called for an illusionistic trellis, about which twined naturalistic grapevines and leaves. Brilliantly rendered birds perched on the trellis against an airy, blue sky.

148. The Children's Room, photograph, ca. 1901. Smithsonian Institution, neg. 85-7818.

The painted birds of the ceiling were brought to life with songbirds kept in four gilded cages. Another delightful novelty in the room was a special kaleidoscope designed by Langley with a triangular tank at the end containing live fish.[18] Nature was used as a model for the color scheme, which was, in turn, viewed as essential to the fulfillment of the room's educational goals. Langley felt that if children had a chance to view natural objects in a comfortable environment, their interest would be spontaneous and genuine, and they would be more likely to learn about the wonder of the natural world. His guiding principle thus became his oft-repeated comment, very loosely paraphrased from Aristotle, that "knowledge begins in wonder." This phrase eventually became the theme of the room and was painted on the transom above the south entrance.[19]

In 1940, when the Smithsonian undertook a major renovation of the Great Hall, the Children's Room space was completely obscured under a sleek, modernist decor as an adjunct to the Lower Main Hall. As part of the new "Index Exhibit," the South Tower Room was used to show the Institution's publishing activities, which were seen as a primary method of "diffusion of knowledge." On display were bound copies of all the Institution's publications from 1846 to 1941. An information desk to assist the visitor was an important new feature.[20]

In response to the attack on Pearl Harbor, the Smithsonian War Committee was established to survey the expertise of the staff and recommend how the Smithsonian could serve the war effort. Barely a year old, the information center in the South Tower Room was converted to office space for the newly formed Ethnogeographic Board. Together with the Smithsonian War Committee, the Board provided geographical, biological, and cultural information on little-known areas involved in the war. As the Secretary stated in his annual report of 1943, "In total war . . . accurate knowledge of obscure peoples and places and other subjects chiefly of academic interest in normal times suddenly becomes of vital importance to the Army and Navy."[21] Experts in the museum responded to queries on subjects as varied as the range of normal head sizes, for use in designing gas masks, and locations of new sources of strategic minerals and plants, such as rubber and quinine. Compiling expertise gained in natural history fieldwork, museum staff members prepared a manual, *Survival on Land and Sea*, which was printed on waterproof paper and distributed to over one million servicemen. Entomologists trained military medical personnel and identified disease-bearing pests to help reduce casualties from insect-borne illness. The Ethnogeographic Board was disbanded at the end of the war, releasing the room for visitor information again.[22]

149. The museum in wartime. Dr. William Dunlap Strong, formerly archeologist for the Bureau of American Ethnology, in the South Tower Room, photograph, 1942.
Smithsonian Institution, neg. 36409.

150. Visitor Information and Associates' Reception Center in the South Tower Room, 1970. Color slide in the Collection of the Office of Architectural History and Historic Preservation.

Exclusively dedicated in 1970 to the Visitor Information and Associates' Reception Center, the South Tower Room was given a Victorian parlor atmosphere. The decor was in keeping with the Victorian feeling of the building renovation. An eclectic mix of furniture and period light fixtures was set against a rich red wall color. To emphasize the history of the Institution, the room was decorated with large-scale copies of vintage photographs of the Smithsonian Building.

151. Roland Cunningham doing preliminary analysis of the Children's Room ceiling painting in the South Tower Room, · photograph by Colin Varga, 1985. Smithsonian Institution, neg. 85-14002-14.

In conjunction with the role of the building as a hub for visitors, in 1988 the South Tower Room became an anteroom to the new visitor information center, connecting it with the recently created Enid A. Haupt garden. Just as the original Children's Room had been designed to create a sense of the wonders of the natural world beyond its glass doors, its restoration provided an ideal transition to the garden. The restored room also symbolized a part of the Smithsonian's history, which recalled the Institution's ninety-year dedication to the education of children.

152. Reopening of the Children's Room, 1988. Color slide in the Collection of the Office of Architectural History and Historic Preservation.

Since the newly restored Children's Room was to serve as an entry and passageway, the Smithsonian did not undertake a re-creation of the cases and original exhibits; it was decided instead to return the room solely to its original decorative design. The elaborate ceiling painting, still intact, was restored. The stenciled wall frieze and the peacock feather displays were re-created based on period photographs of the room, supplemented by Grace Lincoln Temple's design materials and contemporary pattern books at the Smithsonian's National Museum of American History. Restoration returned the room to its position of bringing nature indoors, serving as a passage between the building's interior and the outside.[23]

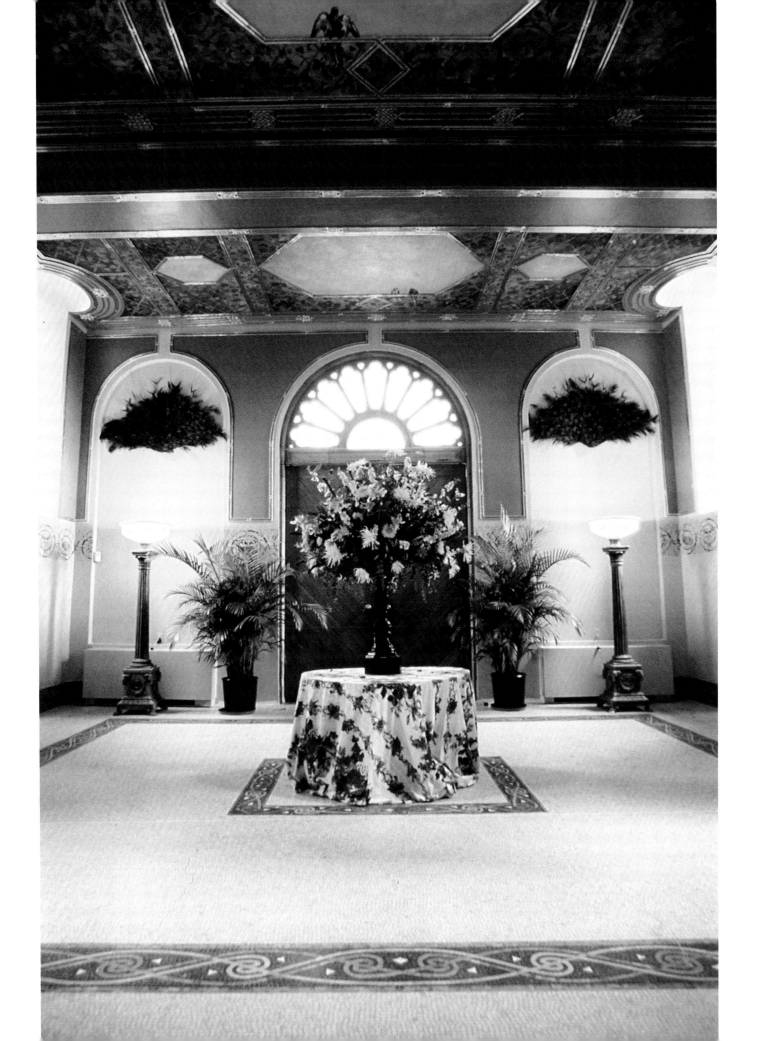

153. Regents' Room, woodcut from William J. Rhees, *An Account of the Smithsonian Institution . . . ,* **ca. 1856.** Smithsonian Institution, neg. 43804-A.

Of the original three rooms of the South Tower, the Regents' Room was the most dramatic. A committee room for the governing board was the one room the Owen brothers believed could be designed in a style truly resonant with the Norman style of the building. David Dale Owen suggested as a model the library of a romantic Norman villa designed by E. B. Lamb, published in Loudon's *Architectural Magazine*.[24] James Renwick, Jr., responded to the suggestion with a narrow but very lofty room. Soaring to about thirty feet, a spidery groin-vault ceiling dominated the space. Black walnut wainscoting encircled the room, which was lit by a large bay window alcove picturesquely set back by a screen of elongated colonnettes.

154. James Renwick, Jr., Regents' chair of ca. 1852, photograph, 1971. Smithsonian Institution, neg. 71-1323.

SMITHSONIAN INSTITUTION

Washington, D.C. 20560
U.S.A.

Dear Contributing Member:

I am delighted to send as your fall benefit the new
Smithsonian publication, <u>The Castle: An Illustrated History of
the Smithsonian Building</u>, by Cynthia R. Field, Richard E. Stamm,
and Heather P. Ewing of the Office of Architectural History and
Historic Preservation.

The Smithsonian Building, a medieval revival structure
designed by James Renwick, Jr., was the original home of the
Smithsonian, housing all of the Institution's operations, as well
as living quarters for Secretary Joseph Henry and his family.
Using historical documents, desk and personal diaries,
contemporary guidebooks, and nearly 200 illustrations -- most of
which have never before been published -- this book documents the
architectural history and evolution of the Smithsonian Building,
affectionately known as "the Castle."

While you read about the history of this extraordinary
building and enjoy the stories of the people who have worked and
lived there, I hope you will be reminded of our gratitude for
your generous and continued support of the Smithsonian
Institution.

                              Sincerely,

                              Robert McC. Adams
                              Secretary

Enclosure

The large table and stately, thronelike chairs visible in the center of the Regents' Room [Fig. 153] were expressly designed by Renwick for the Smithsonian. Each chair was distinguished by architectonic Gothic details, recalling elements of the building's exterior stonework. In the structure's first decade, the chairs designed by Renwick were used in other locations in the building, such as the Lower Main Hall. It is likely for this reason that, although the Regents' Room and its contents were destroyed by the fire of 1865, nine of the chairs survived.[25] When the room was reconstructed after the fire, it was reduced in height by almost half. In the rebuilding of the South Tower, with six rooms taking the place of three, the new Regents' Room lost its original Gothic character, but the chairs returned.

■

After the fire, the soaring groin vault was replaced with a flat ceiling. Supporting this new ceiling were marbleized cast-iron columns, one of which is visible framing the left side of this photograph. The high-relief frieze, consisting of foliated scrolls, which encircled the new room was characteristic of the bold forms of the late 1860s. The Smithsonian had by 1880 accumulated an extensive collection of items relating to the founder, James Smithson. An exhibition of his memorabilia, which included several portraits, books, and the will with the language creating the Smithsonian Institution, was mounted in the Regents' Room.[26]

155. James Smithson's memorabilia in the Regents' Room, photograph, ca. 1880.
Smithsonian Institution, neg. 11810.

After Smithson's remains were ceremoniously delivered to the Smithsonian by Alexander Graham Bell on January 25, 1904, the flag-draped coffin was placed temporarily in what was by that time referred to as the "old" or "former" Regents' Room.[27] The Regents had ceased to meet in the South Tower by 1900, adopting instead a room in the East Wing. The Regents' Room was open to the public for viewing of Smithson's coffin and his personal effects. The coffin stayed in the room for only a year, until its transfer to the newly finished Crypt, but the Smithson exhibition remained until 1912.

By the turn of the century, the architectural firm of Hornblower & Marshall had already modernized the Regents' Room.

156. James Smithson's coffin in the Regents' Room, photograph, 1904. Smithsonian Institution, neg. 15883.

They opened up the space by removing the iron columns.[28] A grand fireplace was constructed using a linear, pale gold brick, which must have become the focus of the room.[29] Furnishings designed for the room included a table and library cases. Contributing to the feeling of a library were Oriental area rugs laid on a darkly stained floor. The chandeliers, equipped with patented Welsbach burners, produced a light comparable with the brilliance and efficiency of contemporary electric lights.[30] The effect was of a warm, convivial atmosphere for a meeting, not unlike that of the library of a large town house of the period.

■

Instead of the elegant, library-like meeting room envisioned by Hornblower & Marshall, the space became by 1920 a repository for the botany library.[31] Serviceably arranged with metal shelves and, somewhat later, fluorescent light fixtures, it was an adjunct to the Herbarium for nearly fifty years, until the library was relocated to the new west wing of the Natural History Building. The view from this vantage point through the medieval oriel window was, during these years, obscured.

157. Botany Library, in the former Regents' Room, photograph, ca. 1965. Courtesy of William Stern, former chairman of the Department of Botany, National Museum of Natural History, Smithsonian Institution.

158. Regents' Room, photograph, 1974. Smithsonian Institution, neg. 74-8521.

As part of Secretary Dillon Ripley's plan to restore the interior of the building to a midnineteenth-century appearance, the Regents' Room was returned to its original use in 1970. The Hornblower & Marshall fireplace was replaced with a richly carved late Victorian mantelpiece in the Renaissance Revival style.[32] The Renwick chairs were returned to the room, and other Gothic Revival pieces were added to enhance the period atmosphere. A new focus was given to the bay window by framing it with dark green velvet curtains. The room acquired a stately grace suitable to its history.

159. Regents' Room, photograph by Richard Strauss, 1992. Smithsonian Institution, neg. 92-16583.

The nineteenth-century theme was augmented in the redecoration of 1987. A new color scheme was introduced, based on Andrew Jackson Downing's *The Architecture of Country Houses* (1850), an important style book contemporary with Renwick's design. Downing stated that the preferred treatment for a Gothic interior was a white ceiling with slightly darker walls in some neutral tint, such as fawn or gray.[33] The walls were accordingly painted a medium gray. The burnt orange carpet of the 1970 renovation was replaced by a gray patterned carpet with a solid border. A Gothic Revival chandelier dated to about 1855 and attributed to Archer & Warner Co. of Philadelphia was hung from the beam in the middle of the room. Brass reproduction light fixtures, like the other decorative details chosen, reflected the period 1850 to 1865.[34]

A portrait of Congressman William Jervis Hough and his family was hung over the mantel in late 1988. Hough, who was the author of the bill that established the Smithsonian, was appointed Interim Secretary of the Institution in September 1846, serving until the Board selected Joseph Henry in December. The placement of this portrait in the Regents' Room was especially appropriate, because it was Hough who introduced the term *Regents* into the legislation.[35]

THE FIFTH FLOOR

The uppermost room of the original South Tower has provided a refuge for those who appreciated its isolated location. In 1852 Joseph Henry moved into this space, seeking some peace from the distraction of the East Range office he had shared with numerous others.[36] Adjacent to this room was a small storage area accessible only through a skylight in the roof. Henry put this gabled attic to good use in 1857, when he ordered the skins being preserved for the taxidermist to be put there. William J. Rhees recounted the transfer:

The Professor had all the skins taken up to the top of the South Tower, where I expect the fleas will have fine times. We rigged up a block at the top of the tower and hoisted up the skins outside, and then put them in the upper room through the skylight. It will be easy to get them down the same way when they are wanted.[37]

During the Civil War, the large top-floor room of the South Tower was used as a repository for the libraries of Beaufort, South Carolina, and Bishop Johns of Fairfax Theological Seminary. The Secretary of War had deposited these collections at the Smithsonian in 1863 for safekeeping until the Union was restored.[38] Ironically, these books were all lost in the fire of 1865, which raged through the South Tower.

When the South Tower was reconstructed after the fire, two floors were created in the top-floor room that Henry had occupied. In the 1880s Robert Ridgway, Curator of the Division of Birds, had his office on the fifth floor of the tower.[39] The room was reached by a flight of stone steps, which Ridgway delighted in bounding up two at a time. The high perch proved more daunting to others, however. Ridgway recalled one visitor,

a very large man, a burly German, opening the door and stepping inside. Breathing heavily, in fact audibly he stopped, mopped his face, then placing his right hand over his heart, as his chest heaved visibly, exclaimed: "Shentlemens, my heart bleeds for you."[40]

With tall windows on three sides, this lofty aerie afforded views of the Washington Monument to the west, the Potomac River to the south, and the Capitol to the east. Throughout the building at this time internal shutters were used for light control, especially in sunny rooms such as this one, where a scientist might be "in danger of being roasted to death," as one curator wryly commented.[41] Ridgway worked in the South Tower from about 1875 to 1895. This was an extremely prolific period, during which he published over 300 articles on birds.[42]

160. Robert Ridgway in his office on the fifth floor of the South Tower, photograph, August 1884. Smithsonian Institution, neg. 92-2158.

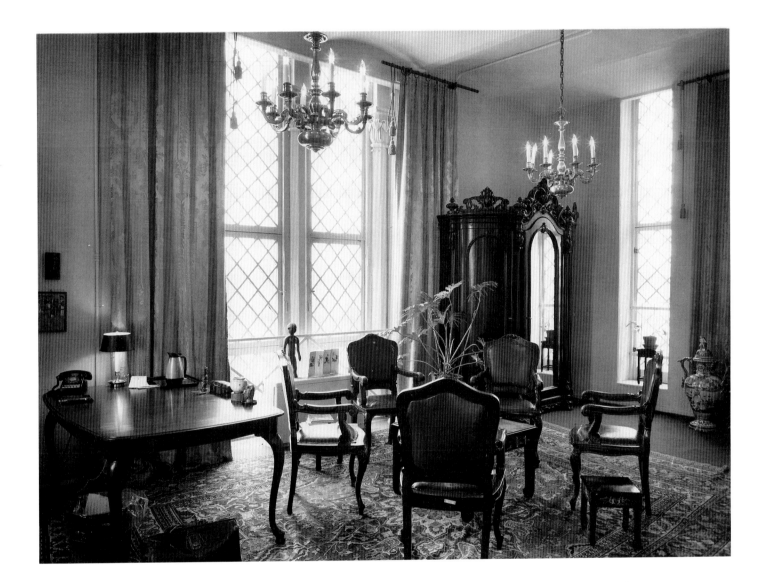

161. Office of Symposia and Seminars, on the fifth floor of the South Tower, photograph, 1972.
Smithsonian Institution, neg. 72-4903.

About one hundred years after Ridgway first occupied the fifth-floor room, Wilton Dillon established it as the headquarters for his Office of Symposia and Seminars. For over twenty years, scholars, foreign and local dignitaries, Native American tribal leaders, and university presidents came for meetings and receptions. Dillon recounted that the aerie setting "excited people's poetry."[43] The furnishings, an eclectic mix of antiques and twentieth-century pieces, helped to create in what had once been a spartan research office the more worldly atmosphere suitable to the broadly international interests of the Office of Symposia and Seminars.

The West Tower: Owls

162. Owls, named Increase and Diffusion, in the West Tower, photograph, 1977. Smithsonian Institution, neg. 87-3904-6A.

Inspired by stories of owls inhabiting the Smithsonian towers, Secretary Ripley set out in 1971 to reestablish their presence.[44] The West Tower [Fig. 166] was selected in 1974 as the roosting place for a group of owls. Because this family did not remain long, a second group was introduced in 1977 [Fig. 162]. These owls were trained at the National Zoological Park before being placed in the tower. Staff members took turns placing dead rats in the tower for the owls, keeping a log of their observations [Fig. 163]. By the end of the summer, there was no sign of this second owl family. One staff member noted in the log:

Fresh "food" and water left. Based upon the disposition of the remains (fur and bones), I remain convinced that we are only feeding the bugs, of which there is a plentiful supply. No sign of recent occupancy by the owls.[45]

The owls never returned, and the tower remains unoccupied. Though empty, it is a valuable witness to the appearance of the interior of the building in its earliest decades. The deeply scored walls and the residue of a rich reddish paint confirm that the interior decorative treatment was designed to mimic the appearance of the exterior building stone.

163. Amy Ballard on her way to feed the owls in the West Tower, photograph, 1977. Smithsonian Institution, neg. 87-3903-3A.

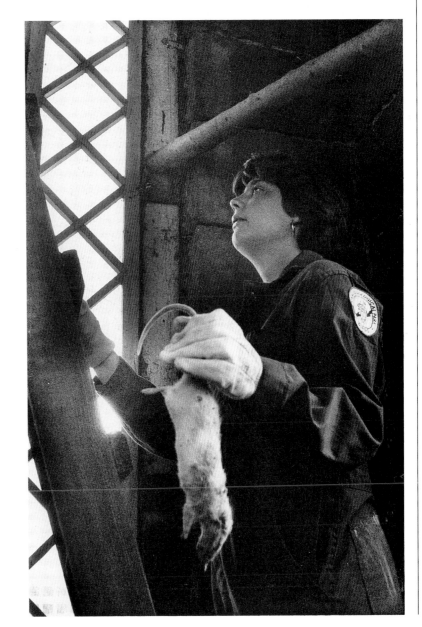

The North Towers

164. James Renwick, Jr., the North Towers, wood engraving by W. Roberts, from Robert Dale Owen, *Hints on Public Architecture*, 1849. Smithsonian Institution, neg. 2534-I.

165. James Renwick, Jr., Church of the Puritans, New York, rendering, 1846. Courtesy of The New-York Historical Society, New York City.

Through the North Towers, visitors could enter the National Museum by any of three doors. The main entrance was announced by a carriage porch, while the other entrances brought visitors in from the east and west. The composition of the two towers, strikingly different in height and design, echoed a traditional church facade. This design was also employed by Renwick in his Church of the Puritans (1846) in New York City [Fig. 165]. Because of this ecclesiastical connection, the uneven tower facade was a most daring design element in an entirely secular building. A large wheel window in the center of the facade reiterated the connection to the Church of the Puritans model. Beneath the window, however, a crenellated carriage porch proclaimed that this edifice was not a church [Fig. 164]; this covered porch, typical of domestic architecture, provided shelter for visitors entering the museum.

166. View from the North Tower, looking west, photograph, ca. 1867. Smithsonian Institution, neg. 31753-G.

The highest of the North Towers figured prominently in stories of the Civil War, frequently invoking the image of Abraham Lincoln reviewing military operations. Mary Henry, Joseph Henry's oldest daughter, noted in her diary that

Virginia the home of Washington is no longer in the Union. . . . We went up on the high tower of the Smithsonian on Thursday morning and saw the secession flags waving in Alex.[andria] while every public building in Washington was surmounted by the stars and stripes.[46]

Not only were grand views possible from the tower but it could also have provided an ideal communications post. One citizen, concerned that the tower was being used to signal to the Confederate troops, urgently sought an audience with Lincoln, who was at the time meeting with Secretary Henry. The visitor

announced that for several evenings past he had observed a light exhibited on the highest of the Smithsonian towers, for a few minutes about nine o'clock, with mysterious movements, which he felt satisfied were designed as signals to the rebels encamped on Munson's Hill in Virginia. Having gravely listened to this information with raised eyebrows, but a subdued twinkle of the eye, the President turned to his companion, saying "What do you think of that, Professor Henry?" Rising with a smile, the person addressed replied, that from the time mentioned, he presumed the mysterious light shone from the lantern of an attendant who was required at nine o'clock each evening to observe and record the indications of the meteorological instruments placed on the tower.[47]

Henry had made meteorology one of the most important activities of the fledgling Institution, creating a network of observers throughout the country.[48] The records were maintained by W. Q. Force in offices on the second floor, one level below Henry's office.[49] Force, who lived in the building, was on hand to take the evening readings.

167. Robert Kennicott and Henry Ulke (standing, l–r), William Stimpson and Henry Bryant (sitting, l–r), photograph, date unknown. Smithsonian Institution, neg. 43604-I.

W. Q. Force was only one of many young men living in the building. Robert Ridgway, a resident in his first years at the Smithsonian, noted that guest rooms were also available for visiting scientists, especially those examining the specimens collected on government expeditions.[50] This tradition became so popular that in 1863 Henry decried the use of the Smithsonian as a hotel:

I have created quite a stir in the Institution by requesting all who have slept in the building except Mr. Meek and DeBeust to find lodgings elsewhere. . . . I do not think it proper to have so many persons without responsibility in the building during my absence; and indeed I have concluded that making the Smithsonian Building a caravansary has been carried a little too far.[51]

It seems unlikely, however, that Henry carried out this mandate. At the time of the fire, less than two years later, there were still a number of people living in the building, primarily in the towers. The reports filed in the days after the fire recording personal losses are important indications of how many were boarders at the Smithsonian.[52]

168. Fire of 1865, heavily retouched photograph by Alexander Gardner, 1865.
Smithsonian Institution Archives, Smithsonian Institution, neg. 37082.

William DeBeust, a machinist in general charge of the maintenance of the building and apparatus, probably occupied the room in the north vestibule that is today the Crypt. One of the workers who placed the stove in the picture gallery in the week preceding the fire of 1865, DeBeust was responsible for saving some of the Stanley paintings. DeBeust's son also apparently lived in the building until Henry ordered him to leave a few months after the fire. The Secretary explained in his desk diary that he "could not suffer his [DeBeust's] son to remain in the building longer. He comes in at all hours of the night and keeps bad company."[53]

Henry W. Elliott, who was Henry's personal secretary, and Henry M. Bannister, a temporary assistant in the museum, shared a room in the North Tower during much of the 1860s. As a precaution against fire, only lights protected in lanterns were permitted in the tower rooms. Elliott explained that "we were also forbidden the use of matches in this room."[54]

In the tower at the northeast corner of the Main Building resided William Stimpson, a naturalist who was classifying material he had collected on the North Pacific Exploring Expedition (1853–56).[55] This tower was always called the Campanile, a reference to an Italian bell tower. Although the Campanile was not damaged by the fire of 1865, firemen broke into Stimpson's room to gain access to the apparatus room and the rest of the main building. Henry in his desk diary wrote:

The firemen on the night of the accident behaved badly. They broke open a room in the NE tower in which the effects of Mr. Stimpson were stowned [sic], plundered his chest drawers and made free use of a quantity of whiskey which had been kept for preserving specimens. They were however repaid for the use of this by the effect of the sulphate of copper which had been dissolved in it. Several of them became deadly sick and would have died had they not vomited freely.[56]

■

169. James Renwick, Jr., Campanile, wood engraving by W. Roberts, from Robert Dale Owen, *Hints on Public Architecture*, 1849. Smithsonian Institution, neg. 2534-H.

170. North Towers after the fire of 1865, looking west, photograph, ca. 1866. Smithsonian Institution Archives, Smithsonian Institution, neg. 74-962.

To salvage the North Towers after the fire, architect Adolf Cluss bricked up a number of the windows and lined the interiors with an additional layer of brick. After the reconstruction, the rooms continued to serve as "studies and dormitories for the investigators in the line of natural history."[57] The painter George Catlin established a studio in the third-floor rooms of the North Towers in the summer of 1872, while his sketches of Indian life were on exhibition in the Upper Main Hall.[58] In late summer Catlin fell ill and was attended for several months by Henry Horan and Joseph Henry's personal servants.[59]

171. Portrait of Fielding B. Meek, photograph, date unknown. Smithsonian Institution Archives, neg. SA-735.

172. Fielding B. Meek, "This Is All the Family I Have," pencil drawing, date unknown. Smithsonian Institution Archives, Smithsonian Institution, neg. 92-15059.

The paleontologist Fielding Bradford Meek [Fig. 171] resided in the building for almost as long as Joseph Henry did, from 1858 until his death in 1876. Like many of the Institution's first scientists, Meek worked without pay, taking his lodging in the building. Until the fire of 1865, he occupied a tiny room under the stairs leading to the balcony in the lecture hall.[60] He had no family at the time of his death, as evidenced by the finely drawn picture of his cat [Fig. 172], plaintively inscribed, "This is all the family I have." Henry wrote that in his last years Meek gradually lost his hearing, and could only be communicated with by means of writing. He gradually withdrew from social intercourse, and devoted his life exclusively to the prosecution of science. He was in correspondence with the principal investigators of the world and although scarcely known in this city his name was familiar to the cultivators of geology everywhere.[61]

(This is all the family I have)

**173. Division of Radiation and
Organisms office in the higher
North Tower, photograph,
December 1929.** Smithsonian
Institution, neg. 18272-A.

By the time of Meek's death, the high towers appear to have been essentially abandoned. No new lodgers seem to have been taken in after Henry's death in 1878; those already in the building remained for a few years. It was not until Charles Greeley Abbot, the fifth Secretary of the Institution, established the Division of Radiation and Organisms in 1929 that the upper reaches of the higher North Tower were again put into use. The purpose of the division was to investigate the effect of solar radiation on weather as well as on living organisms.

The octagonal Flag Tower was of great importance to Abbot throughout his time at the Smithsonian. In 1903, when the tower was accessible only by ladder, he climbed to the top carrying a long telescope to witness the aborted flight on the Potomac of Secretary Langley's flying machine, the *Aerodrome*.[62] For his newly founded division, Secretary Abbot inserted additional floors and an elevator.[63] After his retirement in 1944, Abbot, who lived to be 101 years old, chose the eleventh floor of the Flag Tower for his office. He occupied this room until 1968, when renovations necessitated evacuating the towers.

174. Smithsonian Building, North Facade, showing the lower North Tower without a roof, photograph, ca. 1960. Smithsonian Institution, neg. 32913.

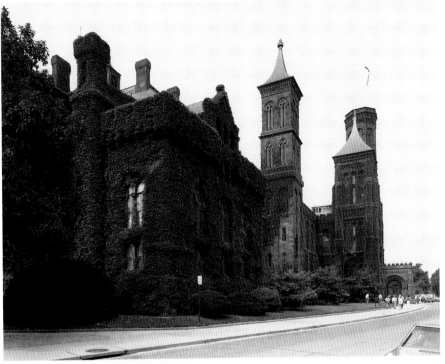

**175. Smithsonian Building
covered in ivy, photograph, 1975.**
Smithsonian Institution, neg. 75-7100.

As part of the renovations planned during the late 1960s, the in-house Committee on Future Building(s) proposed to restore the roof of the lower North Tower, which had been roofless since the fire of 1865. Concurrent with these efforts to improve the appearance of the facade, the committee proposed to install a clock on the Flag Tower. Although a clock had not previously existed in the tower, the committee believed that the numerals inscribed in the stone implied that such had been the architect's intention. In addition, the committee suggested placing bells in the tower to ring the hour, arguing that "the sweet tones of these bells would have a soothing effect upon the foreign scholars in residence behind the brownstone walls."[64] This suggestion was only a part of the efforts to cultivate a collegiate at-mosphere. Ivy, which grew in abundance on the building throughout the 1970s, evoked the ivy-covered walls of historic universities.[65] By designating the Castle as a home for a scholarly center, the committee had found a use for the building that underscored its stylistic, architectural associations.

The towers posed unusual safety problems, and by 1974 the administration had determined that the fifth to twelfth floors of the Flag Tower would be used for storage only.[66] Today the ninth through the twelfth floors remain unused, housing solely the clock mechanism.

THE CRYPT

On either side of the grand north vestibule were two small but lofty rooms, one for the janitor and the other for the Librarian.[67] Both rooms, as well as the vestibule, soared to a height equal to that of the Lower Main Hall, terminating in groin-vaulted ceilings. After the fire of 1865, these rooms were reconstructed at half their original height to provide for an additional floor. Through the rest of the nineteenth century, the rooms served as offices for the building superintendent and watchmen. At the turn of the century, the transfer of the remains of the Institution's benefactor augured a dignified transformation.

In 1901 the Regents of the Smithsonian learned that the Protestant cemetery in Genoa in which James Smithson was buried would be moved to another part of the town.[68] Alexander Graham Bell, inventor of the telephone and a Smithsonian Regent, advocated that Smithson's remains be brought to this country.[69] Bell traveled to Italy to retrieve the remains himself. Pending a decision regarding a fitting memorial, the flag-draped coffin was placed in the old Regents' Room [Fig. 156], where Smithson's personal effects had been on exhibition since 1880.[70]

For the next year, many architects and artists, some of national renown, were solicited to provide designs.[71] The complexity of the proposals varied greatly, including a grand monument [Fig. 176], a gardenlike structure [Fig. 177], and its present room-size configuration. One of the proposals prepared by the local architectural firm of Totten & Rogers showed a monument that would today rival the Lincoln Memorial in size and grandeur. Other artists contacted included the prominent American sculptor Augustus Saint-Gaudens, architect Henry Bacon, and Gutzon Borglum, who later designed and sculpted Mount Rushmore.[72] Borglum submitted an elaborate plan to convert the Children's Room into a classical tomb, incorporating the Italian grave marker flanked by massive classical columns.[73] One can only imagine Secretary Langley's reaction to this proposal to obliterate his Children's Room, which had been open scarcely three years.

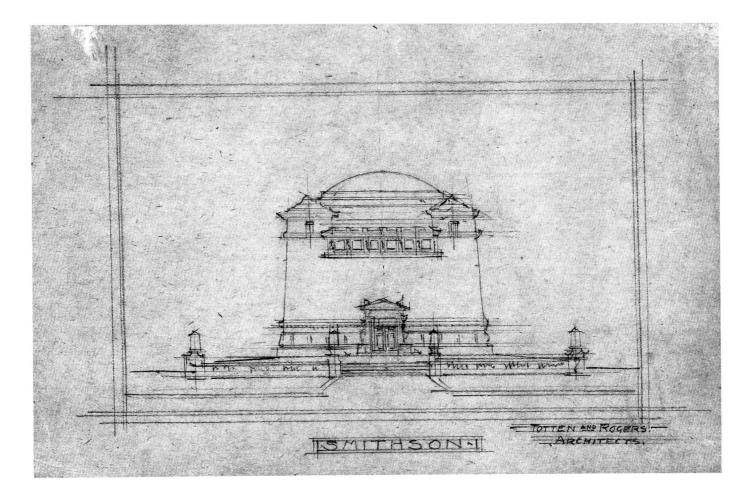

**176. Totten & Rogers, Proposal for
a Smithson memorial, drawing,
1904.** Smithsonian Institution Archives,
Smithsonian Institution, neg. 89-8534.

**177. Henry Bacon, Proposal for a
Smithson memorial, drawing,
1904.** Smithsonian Institution Archives,
Smithsonian Institution, neg. 90-16191.

178. James Smithson's Italian grave site, photograph, 1896–1900. Smithsonian Institution, neg. 82-3195.

Perhaps Borglum's use of the Italian marker influenced Langley to retrieve the marble monument from Smithson's Genoa grave site. Because there was no federal appropriation for the project, all elaborate proposals were set aside. It was decided to convert one of the rooms at the north entrance into a mortuary chapel, incorporating in it the pieces of the Italian grave site.[74] The architectural firm of Hornblower & Marshall, employed at the time in designing the Smithsonian's new museum building, was asked to adapt the room as an interim resting place. Ironically, Smithson has been interred in his "temporary" tomb longer than he had been in Genoa.

179. Hornblower & Marshall, Smithson's Crypt, photograph, 1905. Smithsonian Institution, neg. 16957.

Hornblower & Marshall set out to create a "decorous and fit resting place to contain the existing monument for Smithson and to cover his remains."[75] To establish a somber and contemplative ambience, the architects replaced the windows with yellow and blue stained glass, and the floor with a dark Tennessee marble. They designed a plaster drop ceiling with a deep cove molding, adding a classical feeling. The effect was further dignified by large palms, a traditional symbol of eternal peace.[76] In the presence of the Regents and the Secretary, the casket was carried down to the Crypt from the old Regents' Room.[77] The Crypt was then sealed off by a heavy iron gate fashioned from pieces of the fence that had surrounded Smithson's Italian grave site.

180. Smithson's Crypt, photograph, 1974. Smithsonian Institution, neg. 74-6976.

Significant changes were made to the Crypt in 1973, in an attempt to make the room welcoming. The drop ceiling was removed to reveal the building's Victorian structure, and the iron gate was replaced by delicate half-gates designed to invite visitors into the room. With the installation of a display exhibiting Smithson memorabilia, the atmosphere of veneration was replaced by one of instruction.

The importance of a memorial to James Smithson was borne out by the promi-

nence of the men involved in establishing it. Only when it became clear that Congress would not provide funds for the project was the concept reduced from a monumental architectural or sculptural treatment to its more modest and austere crypt form. Although small and aesthetically spare, this simple room in the Smithsonian's first building is perhaps most fitting, because the Institution itself is Smithson's memorial.

The Building as Symbol

When the Smithsonian Building was designed, it was believed that architecture had the power to communicate the ideas associated with its form. To Robert Dale Owen, who shepherded into existence both the Institution and the building during his two years in Congress, the image had to suggest broad outreach in both the "increase" and the "diffusion" of knowledge:

We must reach the minds and hearts of the masses; we must diffuse knowledge among men; we must not deal it out to scholars and students alone.[1]

To give form to the idea of "increase and diffusion" has been the goal of all Secretaries of the Smithsonian. Secretaries Henry and Baird kept before them the concept of a research institution and a national museum, which were fiscally separate but administratively united. Secretary Langley, however, recognized that the Institution was a single complex of museum and research institution, which he enriched with a zoo, an astrophysical observatory, a nascent art gallery, and a children's room. Secretaries Walcott and Abbot nurtured this combination. In the post–World War II years of national growth, Secretary Wetmore fostered the Smithsonian's research facilities, Secretary Carmichael turned the Smithsonian toward museum education, Secretary Ripley established it as the nation's cultural symbol, and Secretary Adams fostered the extension of the Smithsonian's constituency. The mission, as with all educational institutions, was clearly a cumulative one, which each generation has developed. The enlarged mission of an institution pursuing knowledge and providing it to all the public is close to the vision with which the building was first associated.

181. Official Smithsonian letterhead, engraving, 1892.
Smithsonian Institution Archives, Smithsonian Institution, neg. 60988.

By the turn of the century, the building had become a symbol of the whole Smithsonian. As Secretary Langley said, "In the popular mind the Smithsonian Institution is a picturesque castellated building."[2] For one hundred years, the image of the Castle has been used as the official letterhead of the Institution and the symbol that introduces its educational programs, from tours to television shows. The image of the Smithsonian Building still powerfully communicates the mission of the Institution as it was envisioned and as it continues to evolve.

Notes

Key to Abbreviations

SIA — Smithsonian Institution Archives

OAHP — Office of Architectural History and Historic Preservation

Annual Report for [year] later *Smithsonian Year [year]* — *Annual Report of the Board of Regents of the Smithsonian Institution showing the Operations, Expenditures, and Condition of the Institution [year]*

Chronology

1. E. F. Rivinus and E. M. Youssef, *Spencer Baird of the Smithsonian* (Washington, D.C.: Smithsonian Institution Press, 1992), pp. 129–30.

2. *Annual Report for 1959*, p. 2.

Introduction

1. William J. Rhees, ed., *The Smithsonian Institution: Documents Relative to its Origin and History, 1835–1899*, vol. 1 (Washington, D.C.: Government Printing Office, 1901). Adams, pp. 268–76, for his bill of June 7, 1844; Choate, pp. 280–93; Tappan, pp. 266–68 and pp. 276–80. Only two weeks after receipt of the bill in the House, on February 10, 1845, Owen offered his own substitute bill but was unable to proceed until the Twenty-ninth Congress opened in December 1845, pp. 319, 321–32. For discussion see Marc Rothen-berg, ed., Kathleen W. Dorman, John C. Rumm, and Paul H. Theerman, asst. eds., *The Papers of Joseph Henry*, vol. 6 (Washington, D.C.: Smithsonian Institution Press, 1992), pp. 464–71.

Chapter 1: Evolution of the Design

1. Joel R. Poinsett, *Discourse on the Objects and Importance of the National Institution for the Promotion of Science* (Washington, D.C.: P. Force, 1841), pp. 5–6.

2. Major Richard Delafield to Colonel J. G. Totten, June 3, 1839, Record Group 94, D-531, National Archives, Washington, D.C., "a style not only pleasing to the eye, but . . . in accordance with Collegiate buildings elsewhere." Colonel Joseph G. Totten, Delafield's superior as Chief, Corps of Engineers, was to become head of the Smithsonian Institution Building Committee in 1847. Colonel Totten for Secretary of War Joel Poinsett to Major R. Delafield, June 15, 1839, West Point Archives, no. 164, with the attached letter of Robert Mills to Poinsett, June 1839, endorsing the ogee dome.

3. Robert Mills to the Honorable Joel R. Poinsett, Secretary of War, February 27, 1841, Records of the Office of the Chief of Engineers, Civil Works Map File, Construction 90, no. 5, RG 77, National Archives.

4. Robert Dale Owen to David Dale Owen, August 15, 1845, pp. 5–6, in "Correspon-dence Explanatory of the Details of a Plan of Buildings for a Smithsonian Institute Prepared by David Dale Owen, M.D., and Robert Dale Owen" (Workingmen's Institute, New Harmony, Indiana). As Robert Dale Owen saw it, the Institution would best serve as a teaching establishment, so he directed his brother to "consult utility first, in the various internal arrangements, and let architectural elegance follow as a secondary, though not un-important, consideration." Material in quotes is found in Robert Dale Owen to David Dale Owen, August 15, 1845, pp. 4–5 in "Corre-spondence Explanatory. . . ."

5. Robert Dale Owen to David Dale Owen, August 15, 1845, p. 2, in "Correspondence Explanatory. . . ." "I cannot furnish to you an elevation showing the order of architecture proposed; but Mr. Mills writes me that he se-lected the Anglo-Saxon style; a selection which seems to me judicious, as being solid, imposing, & probably the most economical among ornamental styles." This argument re-flected Owen's familiarity with the work of En-glish writers on architecture Thomas Hope and J. C. Loudon, whom he would later quote in *Hints on Public Architecture*.

6. David Dale Owen to Robert Dale Owen, October 10, 1845, p. 6, in "Correspondence Explanatory. . . ." The descriptive material in the following paragraphs is from this source. William H. Pierson, Jr., in his soon to be pub-lished volume 3 of *American Architects and*

Their Buildings, points out that the wings and ranges were clearly lower than the central building because David Dale Owen described "large" and projecting windows at the east and west end walls of the third story as well as "lofty" windows on the north and south sides.

7. William J. Rhees, ed., *The Smithsonian Institution: Journals of the Board of Regents, Reports of Committees, Statistics, Etc.* (Washington, D.C.: Smithsonian Institution, 1879), p. 4. A letter, from which the quotation was taken, accompanied this project and was printed in H. M. Pierce Gallagher, *Robert Mills, Architect of the Washington Monument, 1781–1855* (New York: Columbia University Press, 1935), "Mills to Robert Dale Owen," appendix, pp. 189–98. Gallagher gave no date for this letter, but in the text—clearly written after passage of the bill on August 10, 1846—Mills referred to Christmas as being three months off.

8. Rhees, *Journals*, pp. 4–6. As a means of advertising the upcoming architectural project, the Regents published the resolution creating the Building Committee in Washington newspapers on September 22, 1846. The architects, however, were already aware of the opportunity. One local builder-architect, William Archer, had submitted his plan and drawings with specifications on September 9. Isaiah Rogers, a highly regarded Boston architect, had come to Washington at the time to obtain the commission if possible. Rogers's presence was recorded in his diaries on September 7, 8, and 9, 1846. We learned of these references through the transcriptions of the diaries, which are in the Avery Architectural and Fine Arts Library, Columbia University. Denys Peter Myers has generously shared the relevant parts of his transcription with the Smithsonian.

9. David Arnot, *Animadversions on the Proceedings of the Regents of the Smithsonian Institution in their Choice of An Architect* (New York: Published for Circulation, 1847), p. 10.

10. Renwick and his heirs kept sketches he made as he was developing his Smithsonian Building entry until their deposit in the Smithsonian Institution Archives in 1992.

11. William H. Pierson, Jr., has identified this drawing as the scheme most closely approximating the final form of Renwick's first submission in November 1846. Drawings Collection Miscellany, Box "Architectural Drawings: Current Files," SIA.

12. John Henry Parker, *A Glossary of Terms used in Grecian, Roman, Italian and Gothic Architecture*, 2d ed. (London: Charles Tilt; Oxford: J. H. Parker; Leicester: T. Combe, 1838). In the copy purchased for the Smithsonian are notes and marks made by Robert Dale Owen. Owen marked the entry for oriel window "committee window," noting at the bottom of the page (p. 89), "We want an oriel window in the Norman style."

13. Robert Dale Owen, *Hints on Public Architecture* (New York: George P. Putnam, 1849; reprint, New York: Da Capo Press, 1978), p. 85.

14. Owen, *Hints*, p. 42.

15. Robert Dale Owen, *Hints*, p. 41. "These were obtained within a bell-tower, of the old Norman form."

16. James Renwick, Jr., "Specification of the Stone and Cutting for the Smithsonian Institution," p. 6, Records of the Office of the Secretary, 1835, 1838, 1846–65, RU 43, Box 1, SIA.

17. Rhees, *Journals*, p. 7. The minutes of the Board of Regents recorded that thirteen plans, two of which were by James Renwick, Jr., were submitted. Twelve are known to us, primarily through mention in Rhees's *Journals*, pp. 4–5, 23, 671–72: those of William Archer, Howard Daniels, William P. Elliot, John Haviland, Robert Mills, John Notman, David Dale Owen, Isaiah Rogers, Owen War-

ren, Joseph Wells and David Arnot, and Renwick twice. The drawings of Renwick, Notman, Rogers, and Warren have survived. The other entries have been lost.

18. Joseph Henry to Harriet Henry, January 20, 1847, Henry Collection, RU 7001, Box 57, SIA. The story of the "tempest" was told in detail in Kenneth Hafertepe's *America's Castle: The Evolution of the Smithsonian Building and Its Institution, 1840–1878* (Washington, D.C.: Smithsonian Institution Press, 1984), pp. 39–61.

19. Rhees, *Journals*, p. 7. "The design includes all the accommodations demanded by the charter, to wit: a museum, 200 feet by 50; a library, 90 feet by 50; a gallery of art, in the form of a T, 125 feet long; two lecture rooms, one of which is capable of containing from 800 to 1,000 persons, and the other is connected with the chemical laboratory; a committee room for the Board of Regents; a Secretary's room; a room for the effects of Mr. Smithson; a janitor's room, &c."

20. Rhees, *Journals*, pp. 12, 17, 18. Henry was elected December 3, 1846 (p. 12). His acceptance letter of December 7 was read into the record on December 14, 1846 (p. 17). He took up his duties on December 21, 1846 (p. 18).

21. Henry to Harriet Henry, December 22, 1846, RU 7001, Box 57, SIA.

22. Henry to Harriet Henry, December 18, 1846, RU 7001, Box 57, SIA. On January 18, Henry was shown Renwick's reduced plan. Acceptance of that plan on January 27, 1847, was recorded in Rhees, *Journals*, p. 29. Other cost-cutting measures were introduced, such as the idea to extend the construction phase so that costs could be met from interest only and a move to cut building costs by more than half, which Joseph Henry described to Harriet Henry, January 27, 1847, RU 7001, Box 57, SIA.

23. This model was found in the building.

According to the catalog card, Joseph Henry's daughter Caroline gave a daguerreotype of this model, located in the Division of Photographic History, to Richard Rathbun for the Smithsonian.

24. Selma Rattner, "Renwick, James," *Macmillan Encyclopedia of Architects*, vol. 3 (New York: Free Press, 1982), pp. 541–48. William H. Pierson, Jr., "James Renwick, St. Patrick's Cathedral, and the Continental Gothic Revival," in *Technology and the Picturesque, the Corporate and the Early Gothic Styles*, vol. 2 of *American Buildings and Their Architects* (New York and London: Oxford University Press, 1978), esp. pp. 215–19.

25. William J. Hough's report on the specifications is found in Rhees, *Journals*, p. 611. For the German and Norman design sources, see Renwick, "Specification of the Stone and Cutting," p. 8, RU 43, Box 1, SIA.

26. Owen, *Hints*, p. 42. "It was judged expedient, that the upper story of the main building should be occupied, in its entire length, by a single apartment, to serve the purposes of a museum. This was effected by running up the staircases within central towers, projecting in front and in rear; these towers harmonizing well with the style adopted; affording small apartments, which were indispensable; and lending themselves to the architectural effect of the structure, both by giving it elevation, which, in its somewhat low and flat site overlooked by Capitol Hill, it wanted, and much increasing its breadth, as seen from the east or west; this latter item being important, inasmuch as the internal adaptations of the main building had given to it a width of but fifty to a length of two hundred feet, and that length again had been more than doubled by the addition of the wings and connecting ranges."

27. Rhees, *Journals*, pp. 599–630.

28. Rhees, *Journals*, p. 7. Meeting minutes of November 30, 1846. See also p. 32 for meeting minutes of February 5, 1847, when the resolution to publish a pamphlet was upgraded to an illustrated treatise.

29. Owen, *Hints*, p. 85. George L. Hersey, *High Victorian Gothic: A Study in Associationism* (Baltimore and London: Johns Hopkins University Press, 1972), pp. 1–43, esp. p. 14. "Loudon believed that 'expression of fitness for the end in view'—i.e., Alison's principal associational test—was a supreme architectural law. On this basis he invented specific meanings for architectural elements . . . saying that these expressed truths about the building's interior, its purpose, the nature of its occupants, its relation to the surrounding landscape, and even its role in local and national life."

30. Owen, *Hints*, pp. 93–98.

31. Owen, *Hints*, pp. 8, 65.

32. Owen, *Hints*, p. 109.

33. Owen, *Hints*, p. 85.

Chapter 2: The East Wing and Range

1. Rhees, *Journals*, p. 597. The Building Committee passed a resolution, February 23, 1847, requesting David Dale Owen to prepare the drawings for the chemical department, for which no payment was to be offered except traveling expenses. Owen, *Hints*, p. 106. Owen stated that the longest distance from the remotest seat to the lecturer's table was forty-four feet.

2. David Dale Owen to Robert Dale Owen, October 10, 1845, p. 17, in "Correspondence Explanatory. . . ."

3. Henry, *Desk Diary of 1849*, April 26, April 27, April 28, April 30, May 1, May 2, May 4, RU 7001, Box 14, SIA.

4. Henry, *Desk Diary of 1850*, January 16, noted the first lecture in the new room. Henry, *Desk Diary of 1849*, July 4, noted the new room could hold 996 persons if each were allotted sixteen inches. Henry, *Desk Diary of 1852*, January 1, mentioned the vaulting. By 1852 the lecture hall had been fitted with gas lights, *Desk Diary of 1852*, April 15. *Desk Diaries*, RU 7001, Box 14, SIA.

5. Henry, *Desk Diary of 1849*, June 3, RU 7001, Box 14, SIA, discussed the fireproof measures taken. *Annual Report for 1849*, p. 61, and Henry, *Desk Diary of 1872*, February 26, marked the time frame for the occupation of these rooms.

6. Owen, *Hints*, p. 79.

7. Rhees, *An Account of the Smithsonian Institution . . .* (Washington, D.C.: Thomas McGill, 1857), p. 33. According to Rhees, research reports for each volume of *Contributions* were printed individually, with separate titles and paging; reports for the year were later collected and bound into volumes. This method allowed the reports to be distributed to scholars interested in particular subjects almost as soon as they were released, without having to wait for the volume to be completed.

8. Benjamin Brown French to Henry, December 4, 1846, RU 7001, Box 8, SIA, in which Henry was promised a house. In Alfred Hunter, *Washington and Georgetown Directory: Stranger's Guidebook and Congressional and Clerk's Register* (Washington, D.C.: Kirkwood & McGill, 1853), p. 48, Henry's address was listed as "w[est] side [of] 10th [Street] w[est] between Maryland Ave[nue] & C S[outh]."

9. Henry to John Torrey, January 15, 1872, RU 7001, Box 4, SIA.

10. Henry to Asa Gray, February 22, 1856, Gray Herbarium, Harvard University.

11. *Annual Report for 1855*, p. 73.

12. Henry, *Desk Diary of 1871*, June 10, RU 7001, Box 15, SIA.

13. The floor plan of 1879 showed two additional rooms adjoining the two bedrooms; their function is not known. No photographs of these inner rooms are known to exist. Peale

did not photograph them, probably because of insufficient light, since there were no windows in one room and only one very small window in the other.

14. The handwritten inscription on the back of the stereo view in the Office of Architectural History and Historic Preservation collection reads: "Misses Henry with compliments of Mrs. T. R. Peale July 31, '62."

15. Helene Von Rosenstiel and Gail Caskey Winkler, *Floor Coverings for Historic Buildings* (Washington, D.C.: Preservation Press, 1988), p. 122.

16. Andrew Jackson Downing, *The Architecture of Country Houses* (1850; reprint, New York: Dover, 1969), pp. 373–74. In addition to explaining how shutters protected a room's fabrics, Downing stated that carpets "are universal in all but the dwellings of the very poor in America."

17. Loris S. Russell, "Early Nineteenth-century Lighting," in *Building Early America*, Charles E. Peterson, ed. (Radnor, Pa.: Chilton, 1976), pp. 198–99. Its name variously spelled "gasolier" or "gaselier," the type of lighting fixture used in the Henry family dining room was designed in the 1850s. The body of the fixture was made to slide up and down on a central, telescoping pipe; the lowest position allowed for igniting the gas. When raised, it could be adjusted to any height desired, held in place by four cast brass "tassels," which acted as counterweights.

18. Florence M. Montgomery, *Textiles in America, 1650–1870* (New York: Norton, 1984), pp. 126–27.

19. Henry to William J. Rhees, August 17, 1865, RU 7001, Box 11, SIA.

20. Mary Henry, *Diary*, January 7, 8, 24, 1863, and July 6, 1867, RU 7001, Box 51, SIA.

21. These photographs were the work of Thomas W. Smillie, the Smithsonian's photog-

rapher from 1871 to 1917. The original glass negatives are in the Smithsonian's Office of Printing and Photographic Services.

22. Downing, *Architecture of Country Houses*, p. 416.

23. Chandeliers similar to the one in Henry's bedroom can be found in *A Reprint of the Historic Mitchell, Vance & Co. Catalog, ca. 1876*, introduction by Denys Peter Myers (New York: Dover, 1984), p. 11.

24. Henry to Alexander Dallas Bache, June 27, 1859, Bache Papers, RU 7053, Box 4, SIA. Lewis Leeds, Consulting Engineer of Ventilating and Warming, New York, to Henry, October 1, 1873, Rhees Collection, RU 7081, Box 5, SIA. Although Henry proposed heating the wings of the building with steam generated from ship boilers, it seems that only the East Wing was supplied with steam heating before the 1873 heating system was installed in the Main Building.

25. Christopher Wilk, *Thonet: 150 Years of Furniture* (Woodbury, N.Y.: Barron's, 1980), pp. 38–39.

26. Thonet's factory exported furniture to the United States in limited amounts during the 1860s. Christopher Wilk, "Thonet and Bentwood," in *Nineteenth Century Furniture: Innovation, Revival and Reform* (New York: Billboard Publications, 1982), p. 122.

27. Mary Henry, *Diary*, January 1, 1863, RU 7001, Box 51, SIA.

28. *Annual Report for 1858*, p. 16. This cloistered walkway was enclosed and decked over in 1858 to create additional space as well as to insulate the building from the cold northwest wind. Mary Henry in her *Diary*, RU 7001, Box 51, SIA, noted on December 24, 1862, that Joseph Henry had presented his daughters with drawing materials.

29. Mary Henry, *Diary*, entries for December 13, 1862; June 12, 1866; August 1, 2, 3, 8, 1866; July 18, 1867; November 23, 1867; December 5, 6, 12, 1867; and March 2, 18,

1868, RU 7001, Box 51, SIA. Mary's self-criticism as an artist, June 12, 1866.

30. Curtis M. Hinsley, Jr., *Savages and Scientists: The Smithsonian Institution and the Development of American Anthropology, 1846–1910* (Washington, D.C.: Smithsonian Institution Press, 1981), p. 101.

31. *Annual Report for 1881*, pp. 43–44. For reasons unknown, Richard was listed as an employee of the Smithsonian in only one volume of the annual reports, that of 1879. The *Annual Report for 1881* contained his necrology.

32. Henry, *Desk Diary of 1872*, February 26, RU 7001, Box 15, SIA.

33. Henry to John Torrey, January 15, 1872, RU 7001, Box 4, SIA.

34. Wooten Desk Co. to H. O. Towles, January 24, 1876, Records of Assistant Secretary Spencer F. Baird, 1850–1877, RU 52, vol. 209, SIA. Towles was the Wooten Desk representative in Washington, D.C.

35. Betty Lawson Walters, *The King of Desks: Wooten's Patent Secretary* (Washington, D.C.: Smithsonian Institution Press, 1969), pp. 2–3, 5.

36. *Annual Report for 1879*, pp. 61–62. According to the floor plan in the 1883 Smithsonian guidebook, the offices in the old laboratory space were then occupied by the chief clerk, corresponding clerk, and bookkeeper. See William J. Rhees, *Visitor's Guide to the Smithsonian Institution* (Washington, D.C.: Judd & Detweiler, 1883), n.p.

37. Memorandum from Rhees to Smithsonian Staff, March 1, 1883, RU 7081, Box 14, SIA. All offices in the East Wing and Range were relocated for the renovation, which lasted a year; the Secretary's office was moved to the new National Museum Building, while the remaining staff were transferred to tower offices and exhibition areas of the Smithsonian Building.

38. Arrangements for the Occupation of

Eastern Portion of Smithsonian Institution Upon Fireproofing, April 1, 1884, RU 7081, Box 5, SIA.

39. Adolf Cluss, "Specifications for the Reconstruction of the East Wing and Range," January 12, 1885, RU 7081, Box 5, SIA.

40. Rhees, ed., *Documents*, vol. 1, p. 466, bill establishing International Exchanges, June 26, 1848.

41. *Annual Report for 1855*, p. 73.

42. *Annual Report for 1891*, pp. 9–11.

43. *Annual Report for 1893*, p. 5. "The plumbing in the eastern part of the building has been thoroughly overhauled, and a suite of dark and damp rooms in the basement on the south side has been transformed into well-lighted and comfortable offices, thus freeing several rooms upon the first floor, needed for other purposes, and making it possible to handle more expeditiously the great number of books passing through the exchange office."

44. S. P. Langley to Edward Clark, Architect of the Capitol, March 6, 1893, Architect of the Capitol Records Office, Subject Files, Box 22. Clark lowered the floor of this area by two feet and enlarged the windows by eighteen inches.

45. *Annual Report for 1893*, p. 5. The date the Exchange was moved from the Smithsonian Building was determined by comparing internal Smithsonian phone books, which are located in the Information Files, SIA.

46. *National Museum Report for 1903*, pp. 257–58. Richard Rathbun here gave a brief history of the gradual installation of electricity in the building.

47. *Annual Report for 1881*, p. 12. The phones communicated through a switchboard in the north tower of the National Museum (now the Arts and Industries Building).

48. *Annual Report for 1914*, p. 616.

49. *Annual Report for 1896*, p. xiii.

50. *Annual Report for 1902*, p. 98.

51. Hornblower & Marshall's original drawings for these cabinets have been preserved in the Smithsonian Institution Archives.

52. The painting visible in the photograph is *Woman with Green Parasol* by Frederick Fursman, 1908, gift of the Fursman Foundation, on loan from the National Museum of American Art.

53. *Annual Report for 1894*, p. 20.

54. *Annual Report for 1884*, p. xxi.

55. *Annual Report for 1913*, p. 20.

56. *Annual Report for 1923*, p. 25.

57. *Annual Report for 1927*, pp. 139–40. Other figures important to the occasion were, on either side of the bust, Alexander Graham Bell's daughter, Mrs. Gilbert H. Grosvenor, and Victor Salvatore, sculptor of the bust.

58. *Smithsonian Year 1966*, p. 11.

59. Geoffrey T. Hellman, *The Smithsonian: Octopus on the Mall* (Philadelphia and New York: Lippincott, 1966), p. 12.

60. Downing, *Architecture of Country Houses*, p. 368.

61. Tahlequah, capital of the Cherokee Nation, is in Oklahoma.

Chapter 3: The Main Building

1. Medieval castles of England and France (eleventh through thirteenth centuries) characteristically included one major communal space, called a "hall" or "great hall," in which all the members of the household could come together.

2. *Annual Report for 1849*, p. 61.

3. Joseph Henry, *Desk Diary of 1850*, February 26, RU 7001, Box 14, SIA. The accident occurred in the evening after Louis Agassiz delivered the first of a series of lectures called "Unity of the Plan of the Animal Creation" in the East Wing. Henry wrote in his diary that "I had left the building a few minutes before with Prof. Agassiz and while at dinner was called to the door with the information

that Prof. J wished to see me. He appeared in a violent state of excitement as well he might considering the narrow escape he had made."

4. *Annual Report for 1850*, pp. 64–65.

5. Henry to Alexander Dallas Bache, October 18, 1854, William Jones Rhees Collection, Huntington Library, San Marino, California.

6. Advertisement of the Second Exhibition of the Metropolitan Mechanics' Institute, Broadside Collection, portfolio 202-2, Rare Book and Special Collections Division, Library of Congress. For Henry and the Mechanics' Institute, see Arthur Molella, Nathan Reingold, Marc Rothenberg, Joan Steiner, and Kathleen Waldenfels, *A Scientist in American Life: Essays and Lectures by Joseph Henry* (Washington, D.C.: Smithsonian Institution Press, 1980), pp. 54–55.

7. "Institute Polka and Schottisch" by Frederic Kley may be seen in the Music Division, Library of Congress. "Smithsonian Polka" by W. Bergmann is in the Information Files, SIA.

8. W. W. Turner to John Russell Bartlett, January 31, 1855, John Russell Bartlett Collection, John Carter Brown Library, Brown University.

9. *Annual Report for 1863*, pp. 55–56. Bannister, Elliott, and Horan were identified from photographs in the Small Print Files, SIA.

10. *Annual Report for 1858*, pp. 14–15. Edward Clark, then "Architect of the Interior Department," supervised the construction. Walter worked closely with Joseph Henry on other aspects of the design of the Lower Main Hall, including helping the Secretary select a pattern for the iron rail that encircled the room at the balcony level. Henry, *Desk Diary of 1858*, March 26, RU 7001, Box 14, SIA. A part of this railing exists in the OAHP collection.

11. Rhees, *Account*, ca. 1864. The reference to the "Feegee Islands" is on page 69,

that to the "mummies" on page 71, and that to the snakes on page 84.

12. *Annual Report for 1867*, p. 106.

13. Henry, *Desk Diary of 1865*, February 11, RU 7001, Box 14, SIA.

14. Richard C. Ryder, "Hawkins' Hadrosaurus: The Stereographic Record," *The Mosasaur* (Delaware Valley Paleontological Society), vol. 3 (1986), pp. 169–80.

15. Henry to S. Baird, July 25, 1874, Baird Papers, RU 7002, Box 25, SIA.

16. *Annual Report for 1881*, pp. 84–85.

17. *Annual Report for 1886*, p. 45. The quotation is from an unpublished manuscript, "Autobiographical Memoir of Mary Jane Rathbun," Mary Jane Rathbun Papers, RU 7256, Box 8, SIA.

18. *Annual Report for 1911*, p. 14. The rationale for this use of the hall was founded in the original 1849 plan. "It is hoped that this hall, which was originally planned for library purposes, may in the near future become available for such use."

19. *Annual Report for 1907*, pp. 30–31.

20. *National Museum Report for 1912*, pp. 15, 39.

21. Blueprints of Hornblower & Marshall's 1914 drawings for the steel stacks are in the SIA.

22. *Annual Report for 1918*, p. 90.

23. *Annual Report for 1913*, pp. 95–96. *National Museum Report for 1915*, p. 13. The relics of James Smithson were also displayed in the hall. *Annual Report for 1912*, p. 130. Secretary Walcott believed that Smithson's relics "aroused a deep interest among those who are acquainted with the history of the Institution." They were moved into the central portion of the Great Hall from the former Regents' Room, which was thought by then to be inaccessible.

24. *National Museum Report for 1919*, p. 59. George H. Sargent, "Life Portraits of American Flowers," *Boston Evening Transcript*, December 28, 1927.

25. *National Museum Report for 1920*, p. 63.

26. *National Museum Report for 1916*, p. 14. These neoclassical fixtures were inverted twenty-four-inch glass (holophane) bowls, pale brownish beige, with color deepening in the thicker parts of the ornamental detail. A great deal of light was produced by the use of eight 60-watt bulbs in each fixture.

27. *Annual Report for 1938*, p. 112, and *Annual Report for 1928*, p. 3. The column remained in place until 1938.

28. *Annual Report for 1939*, p. 14. The committee consisted of Messrs. Mitman (chairman), Foshag, Friedmann, Setzler, and True. They met weekly, beginning in the summer of 1939, according to the *Annual Report for 1940*, p. 13.

29. *Annual Report for 1940*, p. 13.

30. *Annual Report for 1941*, pp. 1, 12–13.

31. *Annual Report for 1955*, p. 4. Quotation from Herbert Friedmann, "The Main Hall, Smithsonian Institution Building and the Exhibition of the James Smithson Relics," a five-page memorandum with a transmittal memorandum from Friedmann as chairman of the Subcommittee on Exhibits Concerning Main Hall, Smithsonian Building, to Dr. Leonard Carmichael, March 30, 1954, Records of the Office of the Secretary, RU 50, Box 45, SIA.

32. J. L. Keddy to Carmichael, December 11, 1959, Records of the Under Secretary (1958–73), RU 137, Box 3, SIA. By late 1959, the Assistant Secretary of the Smithsonian initiated planning for the restoration of this space.

33. G. Carroll Lindsay to S. Dillon Ripley, March 19, 1964, Richard Howland Papers, OAHP Records.

34. In Richard Howland to [John] Ewers, July 14, 1964, RU 99, Box 46, SIA, mention was made of the use of old photographs to provide data for the restoration. Howland to S. Dillon Ripley [through Ewers, Taylor, Bradley], November 5, 1964, RU 137, Box 3, SIA. Frank Taylor to James Bradley, May 17, 1965, RU 137, Box 3, SIA, that the building's spaces were to be used for "public exhibition space; a reception lounge for Friends of the Smithsonian; and for special dinners, lunches, receptions, and galas." References to returning the hall to its original expanse, entailing removing the east and west walls inserted in 1940, are made in Philip Ritterbush to Ripley, October 14, 1964, and April 16, 1965, RU 99, Box 46, SIA. This project was never executed.

35. Richard Howland to S. D. Ripley (through Ewers, Taylor, Bradley), November 5, 1964, RU 137, Box 3, SIA.

36. W. E. Heggman to James Bradley, September 21, 1964, RU 99, Box 41, SIA. The Internal Revenue Service found that the rugs, as part of "the restoration of the building to its original condition," would be permitted to pass through customs without duty.

37. James Goode to Richard Howland, undated memorandum ca. 1971, Smithsonian Building Collection, OAHP Records.

38. Joshua C. Taylor to S. Dillon Ripley, December 22, 1972, RU 99, Box 46, SIA.

39. E. F. Rivinus to S. Dillon Ripley, through Philip S. Hughes, March 31, 1983, OAHP Records.

40. In the summer of 1976, Ralph Schwartz, director of the Historic New Harmony, showed Cynthia Field a window said to be from a building by Robert Dale Owen for which a drawing was said to exist in the Workingmen's Institute, New Harmony, Indiana. The working relationship between Robert Dale Owen and James Renwick, Jr., was apparent in *Hints on Public Architecture*, for

which Renwick produced plates and designed the title page [Fig. 25].

41. *Annual Report for 1854*, p. 70. The National Medical Association, the United States Agricultural Society, the National Musical Convention, the Art Association, and the American Colonization Society all used second-story rooms (see also *Annual Report for 1858*, p. 42).

42. *Annual Report for 1854*, p. 27. Newspaper accounts claimed that the Wagner-Free Institute in Philadelphia, built 1859–65, had modeled its lecture hall after the Smithsonian's. That hall, which still exists, was executed on a much smaller scale, with no balcony, no oculus, and a rectangular floor plan; it was not fan shaped. *The Public Ledger & Daily Telegraph*, May 28, 1860, and *The Philadelphia Ledger and Transcript*, October 24, 1860.

43. *Annual Report for 1852*, pp. 87–88. Alexander (1819–78) was at the time superintending the erection of a military and naval asylum for the District of Columbia and was assigned to the Smithsonian by Colonel Totten of the Corps of Engineers, a Smithsonian Regent. Robert Esau dealt extensively with Alexander's background in his unpublished paper "Fear of Fire: An Investigation into the Fireproofing of the Smithsonian Institution Building, 1846–1890," a copy of which is in the OAHP Records. Esau noted that contemporary Smithsonian reports called Alexander a captain, a mistake that has been repeated frequently in later accounts.

44. *Annual Report for 1856*, p. 234.
45. *Annual Report for 1854*, p. 70.
46. *Annual Report for 1853*, p. 68.
47. *Annual Report for 1856*, p. 231.
48. Joseph Henry, "On Acoustics Applied to Public Buildings," *Annual Report for 1856*, p. 221. Henry read this paper before the American Association for the Advancement of Science in August 1856.

49. *Annual Report for 1858*, p. 42.
50. *Annual Report for 1849*, p. 61.
51. *Annual Report for 1858*, p. 42.
52. *Annual Report for 1868*, pp. 51–52.
53. *Annual Report for 1849*, p. 18. For further information on Robert Hare, consult Charles Coulston Gillispie, ed., *Dictionary of Scientific Biography*, vol. 6 (New York: Scribners, 1972), and Clark A. Elliot, comp., *Biographical Index to American Science: The Seventeenth Century to 1920* (Westport, Conn.: Greenwood Press, 1990).

54. The King portraits had come to the Smithsonian as part of the National Institute collections. *Annual Report for 1858*, p. 41.

55. *Annual Report for 1857*, p. 35.

56. George Catlin, letter of July 1832, printed in *National Museum Report for 1885*, part II, p. 719. Catlin, a painter of Indian life who also worked in the Smithsonian Building during 1872, wrote that "I have, for many years past, contemplated the noble races of red men who are now spread over these trackless forests and boundless prairies, melting away at the approach of civilization; . . . and I have flown to their rescue, not of their lives or of their race (for they are 'doomed' and must perish), but to the rescue of their looks and their modes . . . [so that] phoenix-like, they may rise from the 'stain on a painter's palette,' and live again upon canvas and stand forth for centuries yet to come—the living monuments of a noble race."

57. *Annual Report for 1857*, p. 36.

58. B. S. Alexander to Henry, January 25, 1865. Testimony relative to the U.S. Congress, Senate, Report of the Special Committee of the Board of Regents Relative to the Fire, 38th Congress, 2d session, February 21, 1865, S. Rept. 129, p. 22.

59. Henry to Louis Agassiz, January 31, 1865, Rhees Collection, Huntington Library.

60. Henry to J. M. Stanley, March 11, 1865, RU 33, reel 1, vol. 1, SIA. "All were consumed except the following: Indian Council No. 27, Hunters Escape No. 59, Scalp Dance No. 68, Buffalo Hunt No. 86, Indian of Fleet House No. 97, Indian Chief on Horseback No. 98, Hunters Escape No. 60."

61. Testimony of William DeBeust, U.S. Congress, Senate, Report of the Special Committee of the Board of Regents, pp. 27–28.

62. Henry, *Desk Diary of 1865*, January 28, RU 7001, Box 14, SIA. The work was done with the help of the Secretary of War.

63. *Annual Report for 1867*, p. 102.
64. *Annual Report for 1865*, p. 19.
65. Henry to T. D. Woolsey, August 8, 1862, Woolsey Family Papers, Manuscripts and Archives, Yale University Library. Henry had restricted the use to the directors of public schools, a decision that, he reported to Woolsey, elicited much criticism and many newspaper attacks.

66. *Annual Report for 1866*, p. 17.
67. *Annual Report for 1870*, p. 13.
68. *Annual Report for 1870*, p. 35. "The upper room . . . is entirely free from all hindrance to an arrangement with a view to the best exhibition of the collections."

69. Henry was likely introduced to Hawkins through Robert Barclay, director of the Montrose Natural History and Antiquarian Society in England. Barclay wrote to Henry praising Hawkins, "the eminent Fossil constructive anatomist of London," and alerting Henry to Hawkins's upcoming lecture tour in America. Robert Barclay to Henry, April 14, 1867, RU 26, Box 1, SIA. Within a year Henry had become a solid advocate for Hawkins, writing to Nathaniel Morrison of the Peabody Institute to describe the lecture Hawkins gave at the Smithsonian in June

1868. The audience was "comprised of some of the higher officials of the government and a number of the principal men of science of this city and that all were delighted with his subject and the manner in which he illustrated it, by means of extemporaneous sketches with colored crayons on a large surface of blackened canvas." Henry to Nathaniel Morrison, June 12, 1868, RU 33, Box 3B, vol. 10, SIA.

70. B. Waterhouse Hawkins to Henry, April 10, 1871, p. 3, RU 26, Box 38, vol. 113, SIA.

71. Henry to John Torrey, May 3, 1871, RU 7001, Box 4, SIA.

72. Henry to B. Waterhouse Hawkins, May 8, 1871, RU 7001, Box 4, SIA. Henry wrote that "the appropriation thus far made by Congress for the completion of the building is twenty thousand dollars and at least sixteen thousand dollars of this amount will be required to meet the contracts already made leaving but four thousand dollars with which to commence putting up the cases. We hope however to obtain another appropriation next winter, and, as rapidly as our means will permit, we intend to carry out in a general way the plans you-have prepared."

73. Richard Ryder, "Megatherium: Stereo's Most Photographed Fossil," *Stereo World*, May–June 1984, pp. 20–25, 33.

74. Henry, *Desk Diary of 1871*, February 7, RU 7001, Box 15, SIA. Both Cluss and Edward Clark, the Architect of the Capitol, were actively involved in the planning of this hall.

75. *Annual Report for 1873*, p. 50. The casts of prehistoric animals were moved to the Lower Main Hall as part of a natural history exhibit. *Annual Report for 1874*, p. 121.

76. The whole room was devoted to ethnology, "this being a branch of science attracting perhaps at the present time more attention than almost any other." *Annual Report for 1873*, p. 35.

77. *Annual Report for 1872*, p. 41.

78. Henry to Spencer Baird, July 4, 1873, RU 7002, Box 25, SIA.

79. *Annual Report for 1876*, p. 39. The Tsimshian housefront, catalog no. 410732, was donated by James G. Swan, an employee of the Department of the Interior's Indian Bureau. For a complete discussion, see William C. Sturtevant, gen. ed., Wayne Suttles, vol. ed., *Handbook of North American Indians: Northwest Coast*, vol. 7 (Washington, D.C.: Smithsonian Institution Press, 1990), pp. 271–73.

80. *Annual Report for 1874*, pp. 126–27.

81. "Notice of the Blackmore Museum, Salisbury, England," *Annual Report for 1868*, pp. 408–13. William Blackmore was the founder of the museum, which opened to the public in 1867. Henry stated in the *Annual Report for 1868*, p. 27, that "Mr. Blackmore [is] an efficient and liberal collaborator, who evinces a disposition amply to repay, in returns of specimens and information, the contributions we may be able to make to the stores he has already accumulated." Henry also mentioned receiving Blackmore's advice on museum arrangements and collections in his *Desk Diary of 1872*, April 14, RU 7001, Box 15, SIA.

82. Report on the Operations in the Department of Antiquities, U.S. National Museum, During the Year 1884, Report of Curator Charles Rau, RU 158, Box 4, SIA. The spears were taken off the walls on July 10, 1885. Henry Horan to George Brown Goode, Semiannual Report for July to December 1885, RU 158, Box 22, SIA.

83. *National Museum Report for 1891*, p. 188. "The arrangement in former times was to exhibit all objects of one kind together, classifying them according to function, as has been described. This classification undoubtedly served a good purpose in its beginning, but it had wrought out that purpose, and Dr. Rau de-

clares in his last report [1886] that the collection would be ultimately arranged geographically. Such, therefore, was his intention at the time of his death, and I do but carry it out."

84. *Annual Report for 1891*, p. 188.

85. *National Museum Report for 1891*, pp. 189, 191. Curator Thomas Wilson's Report for FY 1894, RU 158, Box 4, SIA.

86. *Annual Report for 1906*, p. 100.

87. *Annual Report for 1909*, p. 25.

88. *National Museum Report for 1911*, pp. 43–44.

89. *Annual Report for 1928*, p. 29.

90. *Annual Report for 1954*, p. 27.

91. There is no documentary evidence explaining this move, but members of the Department of Botany (in particular Dan Nicolson, who supervised the move) thoroughly photographed the transfer of the Herbarium to the Natural History Building. We are grateful to them for sharing this information with us.

92. Caryl Marsh and Teresa Covacevich Grana, telephone conversations with Cynthia Field, December 2, 1992. The program was funded by United Planning and the District of Columbia Recreation Department as part of the Anti-Poverty Programs of the Johnson years. It ran for the summer of 1965, using the hall in the daytime for the children's programs and in the late afternoon and evening for workshops training staff from fifty recreation centers.

93. *The Washington Post*, October 19, 1970, OAHP Records.

94. N. Patrick Shealy, Acting Director, Project Coordination Staff for General Services Administration, to Charles Stover of Chatelain, Gauger and Nolan, October 17, 1966, Chatelain Papers, Smithsonian Building Collection, OAHP Records. Established in 1930, Chatelain, Gauger and Nolan specialized in commercial and public buildings in the Washington, D.C., area. The firm was selected in

spring 1965 from a list of architects furnished by the General Services Administration. S. Dillon Ripley to the Hon. Lawson B. Knott, Jr., Acting Administrator of GSA, copy dated May 26, of letter dated May 25, 1965, RU 137, Box 3, SIA.

95. Richard Howland to Phil Ritterbush, July 15, 1966, p. 3, RU 99, Box 46, SIA.

Chapter 4: The West Wing and Range

1. Owen, *Hints*, p. 86.

2. Henry, *Desk Diary of 1852*, February 9, RU 7001, Box 14, SIA.

3. Diary of Francis Ormand French (1837–93), December 31, 1851, Benjamin Brown French Family Papers, Manuscript Division, Library of Congress. Francis was the son of Benjamin Brown French, the Grand Master of Masons for the District of Columbia, who presided over the laying of the Smithsonian Building cornerstone. The father served as Assistant Secretary under William Jervis Hough during the first months of the Institution's history, extending to Joseph Henry the invitation to become Secretary. He was later Commissioner of Public Buildings and Grounds, a position that included supervising the maintenance and design of the Smithsonian grounds.

4. Henry Horan to George Brown Goode, Semi-annual Report, May 31, 1882, Records of the U.S. National Museum, 1881–1964, Curators' Annual Reports, RU 158, Box 22, SIA. Owen, *Hints*, pp. 84–85, wrote a footnote on the clerestory in a "Norman or Gothic cathedral" in reference to the West Range.

5. *Annual Report for 1857*, p. 31.

6. Downing, *Architecture of Country Houses*, p. 446.

7. *Annual Report for 1860*, p. 53.

8. *Annual Report for 1866*, p. 14. *National Museum Report for 1896*, p. 301.

9. *Annual Report for 1868*, p. 34.

10. Henry, *Desk Diary of 1871*, April 11, RU 7001, Box 15, SIA. "The large room formerly occupied by the library having had the old and decayed floor replaced with iron girders and brick arches will be ready for the meeting of the National Academy on Tuesday one week from today. The outer range will be used as the meeting room for the committee of the academy."

11. Henry, *Desk Diary of 1871*, April 11, RU 7001, Box 15, SIA.

12. Rexmond C. Cochrane, *The National Academy of Sciences: Its First Hundred Years, 1863–1963* (Washington, D.C.: National Academy Press, 1978). The use of the room is referred to on page 17.

13. *Annual Report for 1863*, pp. 55–56.

14. *Annual Report for 1871*, p. 38. The floor was raised eighteen inches. Henry, *Desk Diary of 1871*, February 23, RU 7001, Box 15, SIA.

15. Richard Rathbun, "The National Gallery of Art," *U.S. National Museum Bulletin 70* (Washington, D.C., 1909), p. 32. See also the entry for Guizot in *Enciclopedia Universal Ilustrada*, vol. 27 (Madrid, 1925), pp. 311–13.

16. *Annual Report for 1869*, p. 26.

17. *National Museum Report for 1885*, pt. 2, p. 803. Henry wrote to Shindler that "you can have wall-room at the Institution for your Indian portraits though if placed here they will be at your own risk." Henry to A. Z. Shindler, May 18, 1870, Records of the Secretary, Outgoing Correspondence for December 1869–May 1870, RU 33, Box 6, SIA. We are grateful to Paula Fleming, National Anthropological Archives, for leading us to this reference.

18. Rathbun, "National Gallery of Art," pp. 70–71. These sculptures and several portrait busts from the art collection were loaned to the Corcoran Gallery of Art in 1874 for safekeeping.

19. Henry, *Desk Diary of 1858*, January 4, RU 7001, Box 14, SIA. Glass doors, given by the Secretary of the Interior, enclosed the cloisters.

20. Thomas W. Smillie, "History of the Department of Photography," July 1906, Records of Assistant Secretary in charge of the U.S. National Museum (Richard Rathbun), 1897–1918, RU 55, Box 20, SIA. Henry, *Desk Diary of 1870*, March 24, RU 7001, Box 15, SIA. Both sourses stated that the Regents' Room was used for photography before this studio was developed. Figure 121 was inscribed by William H. Holmes, "In 1871–1872, I studied photography with Mr. Smillie in the room next this, in the Smithsonian Building."

21. Rhees, *Visitor's Guide*, ca. 1890, p. 38.

22. *Annual Report for 1881*, p. 105. "The fitting up of the west range of the Smithsonian building for the reception of alcoholic vertebrates—a work now nearly completed—will enable the curator of this department to revolutionize its arrangement during the coming year."

23. Henry Horan to George Brown Goode, Semi-annual Report, May 31, 1882, RU 158, Box 22, SIA.

24. *Annual Report for 1888*, pp. 17–18. Although the previous scheme had employed a stone flagging for the floor, it had been set in a wooden framework supported by wooden beams. The work carried out by Cluss & Schulze, which provided a wooden floor, was nonetheless considered fireproof because the supporting members consisted of iron beams and brick vaulting.

25. Cluss & Schulze to Langley, April 10, 1888, Records of the Office of the Secretary for 1882–90, Incoming Correspondence, RU 30, Box 3, SIA. This letter is inscribed on top "Do Nothing."

26. Cluss to Edward Clark, [undated, ca.

1890], Architect of the Capitol Records Office, Subject Files, Box 22.

27. *Annual Report for 1891*, p. xii. For information on Edward Clark, see Henry F. Withey and Elsie Rathburn Withey, *Biographical Dictionary of American Architects (Deceased)* (Los Angeles: New Age, 1956), p. 121. Clark first worked for the Smithsonian in 1855, when he supervised the construction of the museum hall for Thomas Ustick Walter (see note 10, chap. 3). He was subsequently involved in the renovation of the Upper Main Hall into a museum in 1870. In 1880 his advice was sought about the interior decoration of the new National Museum Building. Consultation with Clark continued through the 1890s, concerning efforts to increase light in the East Wing, to investigate the structural soundness of the South Tower, to fit up the building with an archives, and other issues. All Clark's incoming letters are in the Architect of the Capitol Records Office, Subject Files, Box 22.

28. *National Museum Report for 1893*, pp. 164–66. The marine invertebrates had actually been put on display in 1887. However, because of the closing of the West Range for fireproofing, the West Wing was inaccessible. The exhibition was probably only open for one or two years in 1889–90. *National Museum Report for 1887*, pp. 128–29. *National Museum Report for 1888*, p. 175. *National Museum Report for 1889*, p. 381.

29. *National Museum Report for 1897*, p. 53. *Report of the United States Government Exhibit at the Tennessee Centennial Exposition Nashville* (Washington, D.C.: Government Printing Office, 1901), plates 30, 31.

30. *National Museum Report for 1901*, pp. 65, 187–88.

31. *National Museum Report for 1901*, p. 66.

32. *National Museum Report for 1902*, pp. 59–60.

33. *National Museum Report for 1913*, p. 46.

34. From an undated pamphlet entitled "The Star Spangled Banner" (Washington, D.C.: Smithsonian Institution), copy in the Smithsonian Building Collection, OAHP Records.

35. Charles Walcott to Elliott Woods, October 10, 1908, Office of the Secretary for 1907–24, RU 45, Box 79, SIA. Congress transferred the statue to the Smithsonian because of concern over its deterioration as a result of exposure.

36. "Draft of the Minutes of the first meeting of the Advisory Committee on Painting and Sculpture for the National Gallery of Art, held April 16, 1908," RU 45, Box 78, SIA.

37. *National Museum Report for 1963*, p. 21.

38. *National Museum Report for 1889*, p. 301.

39. *National Museum Report for 1938*, p. 68.

40. *National Museum Report for 1943*, pp. 7–8.

41. *Annual Report for 1888*, pp. 17–18. These fireproofed rooms furnished offices for the Department of Marine Invertebrates and were later turned over to Graphic Arts.

42. *Annual Report for 1955*, p. 33.

43. *Annual Report for 1956*, pp. 4, 38.

44. *National Museum Report for 1959*, p. 30.

45. Minutes of the Meeting of the Committee on Future Building(s), September 3, 1965, Smithsonian Building Collection, OAHP Records. During the early planning, a suggestion was made to open the lounge and dining room for public viewing but close it to the public during meals, on the ground that this was "a common practice at colleges and universities."

46. James Bradley to J. Rowland Snyder, Director of Design Division, Public Build-

ing Service, General Services Administration, June 24, 1966, RU 99, Box 46, SIA.

47. A. F. Michael to R. H. Howland, June 17, 1970, RU 99, Box 384, SIA. In a telephone conversation with Cynthia Field on December 1, 1992, Richard Howland stated that the ceiling treatment was chosen because Sainte-Chapelle was deemed an appropriate source in terms of period of restoration and proportion of height to width.

48. James Goode correspondence and memos relating to the Escutcheons, 1971, Smithsonian Building Collection, OAHP Records.

49. S. Dillon Ripley to John T. Fesperman, October 7, 1971, RU 99, Box 480, SIA.

50. Mary Grace Potter to Robert Mason, December 19, 1974, attached to letter from Potter to James Goode, February 24, 1975, Records of the Secretary, 1975, Box 8, SIA. In conjunction with the renovation of the Great Hall in 1986–87, a long ramp was installed in the West Range, providing wheelchair access to the Commons.

Chapter 5: The Towers

1. Henry, *Desk Diary of 1850*, April 23, RU 7001, Box 14, SIA. Henry believed that "the building would be improved by so doing."

2. *Annual Report for 1864*, p. 38.

3. Mary Clemmer Ames, *Ten Years in Washington: Life and Scenes in the National Capital, as a Woman Sees Them* (Cincinnati: Queen City Publishing, 1874), p. 541.

4. Henry to Asa Gray, November 6, 1852, Gray Herbarium, Harvard University. Henry was in the South Tower office from 1852 to about 1858, when he moved to the North Towers.

5. *National Museum Report for 1903*, p. 218.

6. *Annual Report for 1867*, p. 103.

7. St. Dunstan Correspondence, 1978–84, Smithsonian Building Collection, OAHP Records.

8. Rhees, *Account*, p. 18.

9. Rhees, *Visitor's Guide*, ca. 1890, p. 72. Commodore Elliott, who brought the sarcophagus to the United States in 1839, wrote to the president and directors of the National Institute, April 8, 1845, explaining why Jackson had refused the honor.

10. Langley to Rathbun, November 30, 1898, RU 55, Box 17, SIA.

11. F. W. True to Joseph C. Hornblower, October 10, 1899, RU 55, Box 17, SIA. At the turn of the century, Hornblower & Marshall were also involved in alterations to the Arts and Industries Building and Holt House at the National Zoological Park. By 1904 they were preparing designs for Smithson's Crypt in the Smithsonian Building and were in the midst of two major Smithsonian construction projects: the National Museum of Natural History on the National Mall and the first Small Mammal House at the National Zoological Park.

12. Hugo Mulertt to Frederick W. True, January 26, 1901, RU 55, Box 17, SIA. Mulertt designed the aquarium.

13. J. S. Goldsmith to J. E. Watkins, April 26, 1900, RU 55, Box 17, SIA. On the role of the architects, see Hornblower & Marshall to Rathbun, October 19 and October 28, 1899, Records of the Office of the Secretary, 1891–1906, RU 31, Box 35, SIA.

14. For biographical information on Grace Lincoln Temple, see Linda NeCastro, "Grace Lincoln Temple and the Smithsonian's Children's Room of 1901" (M.A. thesis, Bryn Mawr College, 1988). See also Jessie Fant Evans, "Pioneer Career Woman Here Is Authority in Art World," *Washington Star*, December 29, 1940.

15. See Temple's drawings in the Clark Collection, cat. 258604.2, Division of Political History, National Museum of American History, Smithsonian Institution.

16. Owen Jones, *The Grammar of Ornament*, first published in England, 1856; in America, 1880 (London: Day and Son, 1856; reprint, New York: Portland House, 1986). Among Temple's papers are study sketches and tracings of the Egyptian and the Assyrian and Persian pages taken directly from Jones's *Grammar*. The fact that she looked to Jones for study in the history of ornament reinforces the idea that she probably used the Celtic pages in *Grammar of Ornament* for decoration in the Children's Room. Furthermore, the mosaic floor was described as "Celtic" by the numerous newspaper accounts of the room's decoration. (Clippings in RU 55, Box 17, SIA.) Although no direct documentation for Temple's role in the floor's design exists, her involvement seems very likely.

17. Langley to Frederick W. True, June 18, 1900, RU 55, Box 17, SIA.

18. Langley to True, December 18, 1900, RU 55, Box 17, SIA.

19. *Annual Report for 1901*, pp. 554–55. See also Mary McCutcheon, "The Children's Room at the Smithsonian: 1901 to 1939," *Curator*, vol. 35, no. 1 (March 1992), p. 12.

20. *Annual Report for 1941*, p. 13.

21. *National Museum Report for 1943*, p. 2.

22. Wendell Clark Bennett, "The Ethnogeographic Board," *Smithsonian Miscellaneous Collections*, vol. 107, no. 1 (Washington, D.C.: Smithsonian Institution, 1947). See also *Annual Report for 1945*, pp. 459–72. Strong, former anthropologist of the Bureau of American Ethnology, returned in 1944 to his professorship at Columbia University. We would like to thank Pam Henson for leading us to these sources and sharing her work with us.

23. Information on the restoration is in the Smithsonian Building Collection, OAHP Records.

24. David Dale Owen to Robert Dale Owen, October 10, 1845, pp. 11–12, in "Correspondence Explanatory. . . ." "If it were thought desirable to finish and fit up an apartment in the building in character with the times whence the style of architecture is derived, it could be done, at small expense, in the Committee room. The ceiling might be ribbed, the ribs of oak, with carved bosses at their intersection; and the ceiling arched on the sides. . . . Other details will suggest themselves; & some may be gathered from the description of a Norman villa by E. B. Lamb, given in Loudon's *Architectural Magazine*, vol. 2, whence most of the above was derived."

25. Records of the Office of the Secretary, 1835, 1838, 1846–65, RU 43, Box 1, SIA. Renwick's specifications called for eighteen chairs: "Eighteen heavily carved arm chairs and one heavily carved table in the Norman style, will be carved for the Regents' room, from the best black walnut, varnished 4 coats and polished. The whole to be carved according to the designs and directions of the architect." There is no evidence of whether all eighteen were delivered; however, the nine Renwick chairs still existing match this description.

26. *Annual Report for 1880*, p. 4. Relics the Smithsonian had collected during the first years of its history were placed on display in the Regents' Room in 1857. *Annual Report for 1857*, pp. 34–35. These items were destroyed in the fire of 1865, and the Smithsonian began anew collecting Smithson memorabilia. It is of interest that in Owen, *Hints*, plate facing p. 105, the second story of the small Campanile, on the northeast corner of the Main Building, was designated to receive Smithson's effects.

27. Joseph C. Hornblower to Langley, May 22, 1900, Records of the Office of the Secretary (Samuel P. Langley), 1891–1906, RU 31, Box 35, SIA.

28. "More Room at the Smithsonian," *The Evening Star*, May 27, 1899, p. 13, copy in the Smithsonian Building Collection, OAHP Records.

29. Hornblower to Rathbun, April 23, 1900, RU 31, Box 35, SIA. The firm recommended the fireplace be "made in 'old gold' brick (similar to the exterior of W. J. Boardman's house), with two shelves of red stone." The Boardman House of 1893, at 1818 P Street, NW, was one of Hornblower & Marshall's most important commissions. See also Anne E. Peterson, *Hornblower and Marshall, Architects* (Washington, D.C.: Preservation Press, 1978), p. 18.

30. Roger W. Moss, *Lighting for Historic Buildings: A Guide to Selecting Reproductions* (Washington, D.C.: Preservation Press, 1988), p. 184. The Welsbach burner was patented in 1885 and in use in this country from 1890 until its replacement by electricity.

31. The Herbarium was moved into the Upper Main Hall in 1910. *Annual Report for 1910*, p. 29. The library was first mentioned in 1919. *Annual Report for 1919*, p. 92.

32. Richard Howland to Philip Ritterbush, July 15, 1966, Records of the Office of the Secretary (S. Dillon Ripley), 1964–71, RU 99, Box 46, SIA. See also accession card, SI.65.88, OAHP "Castle" Collection.

33. Downing, *Architecture of Country Houses*, p. 372.

34. The reproduction fixtures were based on examples from the 1856 lighting catalog of Starr, Fellows & Co., of New York, copy in OAHP Records.

35. Rhees, *Documents*, pp. 423–27. For further information, see entry on Hough in *Biographical Directory of the American Congress, 1774–1971* (Washington, D.C.: U.S. Government Printing Office, 1971). Hough was from New York, where the term *Regents* has been in continuous use for the governors of the University of the State of New York, as ex-

plained in *The Papers of Joseph Henry*, vol. 1, p. 10.

36. Henry, *Desk Diary of 1850*, February 23, RU 7001, Box 14, SIA. Henry noted that he occupied Jewett's office, which was on the second floor of the East Range (Henry, *Desk Diary of 1849*, November 1 and 4, RU 7001, Box 14, SIA). Henry described the move of his office in a letter to Asa Gray, November 6, 1852. Gray Herbarium, Harvard University. By 1860 the Secretary's offices were in the North Tower. Rhees, *Account*, 1859, p. 13.

37. Rhees to Spencer F. Baird, September 1, 1857, Baird Papers, RU 7002, Box 31, SIA.

38. U.S. Congress, Senate, Report of the Special Committee of the Board of Regents, p. 3.

39. Harry Harris, "Robert Ridgway, with a Bibliography of His Published Writings," reprinted from *The Condor*, vol. 30 (January 1938), pp. 15–20. Ridgway's association with the National Museum began in 1867 on the geological survey of the fortieth parallel, as a zoologist collecting specimens. Spencer Baird recommended him to accompany Clarence King, U.S. geologist, on the survey. Ridgway had come to Baird's attention at a very early age; the aspiring ornithologist had initiated a correspondence with Baird on the identification of birds. Ridgway enclosed with each letter a carefully colored drawing of the bird in question, sometimes including specimens as well.

40. Harris, "Robert Ridgway," p. 32.

41. Otis Mason to Richard Rathbun, June 2, 1902, Records of the Administrative Assistant of the National Museum, 1882–1914, RU 198, Box 1, SIA. This letter was written two decades after the Ridgway photograph and with specific reference to a different office, but its relevance to these problems of excessive sun was likely. Awnings were used at the same time on the exterior.

42. Robert Ridgway to Spencer Baird, December 6, 1875, RU 7002, Box 32, SIA. *National Museum Report for 1895*, pp. 55–56, stated that he was writing primarily out of his home. For more information, see *Annual Report for 1929*, pp. 20–21.

43. Wilton Dillon to Richard Stamm, interview, October 7, 1992.

44. S. Dillon Ripley to Dr. Alexander Wetmore, November 4, 1971. The history of owls in the building is contained in Wetmore's response of November 15, 1971. Both records in RU 99, Box 509, SIA.

45. James Dodd, entry for September 9, 1977, Owl Record, Smithsonian Building Collection, OAHP Records.

46. Mary Henry, *Diary*, April 15, 1861, RU 7001, Box 51, SIA.

47. William B. Taylor, "A Memoir of Joseph Henry, A Sketch of His Scientific Work," *Bulletin of the Philosophical Society* (Philadelphia, 1879), pp. 324–25.

48. For a detailed discussion of the Smithsonian's meteorological project, see James Rodger Fleming, *Meteorology in America, 1800–1870* (Baltimore and London: Johns Hopkins University Press, 1990), ch. 4.

49. U.S. Congress, Senate, Report of the Special Committee of the Board of Regents, p. 26. Force helped remove these records during the fire of 1865, ensuring their survival; as he testified afterward, "I remained in the rooms, directing what was most important to be removed, until driven out by the smoke, and then left by way of a ladder from the north portico, on which stones were then falling from the walls of the building."

50. Harris, "Robert Ridgway," p. 31.

51. Henry to Spencer Baird, August 24, 1863, RU 7002, Box 25, SIA.

52. U.S. Congress, Senate, Report of the Special Committee of the Board of Regents.

53. Henry, *Desk Diary of 1865*, March 15, RU 7001, Box 14, SIA.

54. U.S. Congress, Senate, Report of the Special Committee of the Board of Regents, p. 33.

55. Records of the North Pacific Exploring Expedition Collection, 1852–61 and undated, RU 7253, Box 1, SIA.

56. Henry, *Desk Diary of 1865*, January 25, RU 7001, Box 14, SIA.

57. *Annual Report for 1871*, p. 38.

58. Henry, *Desk Diary of 1872*, September 26, RU 7001, Box 15, SIA. The Catlin sketches were installed in February. Henry, *Desk Diary of 1872*, February 27, RU 7001, Box 15, SIA.

59. At the time of his death, Catlin had returned to his home in New Jersey. As Henry explained in the *Annual Report for 1872*, p. 41, "Unfortunately, in passing between the Institution and his boarding place which were separated by the distance of more than a mile, he exposed himself to the heat of the unusually warm summer, and was seized with a malady which terminated his eventful life on the 23rd of December, 1872."

60. U.S. Congress, Senate, Report of the Special Committee of the Board of Regents, p. 31.

61. *Annual Report for 1877*, pp. 9–11.

62. Charles Abbot to S. Dillon Ripley, August 6, 1968, RU 99, Box 213, SIA.

63. *Annual Report for 1929*, p. 9.

64. R. P. Wunder to S. Dillon Ripley, May 18, 1965, RU 99, Box 46, SIA.

65. When it was removed in 1982 because of damage to the building stone, the Department of Botany determined that most of the ivy was about twenty years old. Nineteenth-century photographs showing the building with ivy indicate that there was precedent for it. In 1900 Secretary Langley received a gift of "a slip of ivy from the tomb of James Smithson at Genoa." He wrote to the donor that he would "have it carefully nursed for a time and planted about the Smithsonian building."

Langley to Harriet E. Wells, May 31, 1900, RU 34, Box 9, SIA.

66. David Billings to Kenneth Shaw through Robert Burke, December 27, 1974, Smithsonian Building Collection, OAHP Records.

67. Owen, *Hints*, plate facing p. 105.

68. *Annual Report for 1901*, p. xix.

69. *Annual Report for 1902*, p. xiv.

70. *Annual Report for 1904*, p. 10.

71. These proposals were discussed in detail in Richard Stamm, "The History of Smithson's Crypt," unpublished ms, Smithsonian Building Collection, OAHP Records.

72. Henry Bacon to Langley, April 29, 1904, RU 7000, Box 4, SIA. Saint-Gaudens declined to participate in the project, stating that the sum was insufficient for a monument. Augustus Saint-Gaudens to Langley, March 28, 1904, James Smithson Collection, 1796–1951, RU 7000, Box 4, SIA.

73. Gutzon Borglum to Alexander Graham Bell, October 8, 1904, Alexander Graham Bell Papers from the Gilbert H. Grosvenor Collection, Manuscript Division, Library of Congress.

74. The elements from the grave site included the coffin-shaped marble marker, the fence, and a commemorative plaque originally executed in bronze by William Ordway Partridge in 1896. This plaque, which was stolen in 1900, was replaced with a marble copy. Stamm, unpublished ms., OAHP Records.

75. Joseph C. Hornblower to Langley, January 24, 1905, RU 7000, Box 5, SIA.

76. Franz S. Meyer, *Meyer's Handbook of Ornament* (1894; reprint, London: Omega, 1987), p. 48.

77. *Annual Report for 1905*, pp. 6–7.

The Building as Symbol

1. Rhees, *Documents*, p. 348.

2. *Annual Report for 1901*, p. 53.

Bibliography

Primary Sources

The files of the Office of Architectural History and Historic Preservation contain many items collected over some fifteen years by Richard Howland, James Goode, and Cynthia Field from Smithsonian sources and others. Published sources invaluable for the primary information they yielded were

Annual Report of the Board of Regents of the Smithsonian Institution, abbreviated as *Annual Report for [year]*. Washington, D.C.: Smithsonian Institution, 1850–1991.

Henry, Joseph. Letters and diaries, unpublished, Smithsonian Institution Archives, RU 7001, Box 15.

Henry, Mary. Letters and diaries, unpublished, Smithsonian Institution Archives, RU 7001, Box 51.

Report of the United States National Museum, abbreviated as *National Museum Report for [year]*. Washington, D.C.: Smithsonian Institution, 1884–1964.

Rhees, William J., ed. *The Smithsonian Institution: Journals of the Board of Regents, Reports of Committees, Statistics, Etc.* Washington, D.C.: Smithsonian Institution, 1879.

———. *The Smithsonian Institution: Documents Relative to its Origin and History, 1835–1899*. 2 vols. Washington, D.C.: Government Printing Office, 1901.

Additional Sources

Alexander, Edward P. *Museum Masters: Their Museums and Their Influence*. Nashville, Tenn.: American Association for State and Local History, 1983.

Ames, Mary Clemmer. *Ten Years in Washington: Life and Scenes in the National Capital, as a Woman Sees Them*. Cincinnati: Queen City Publishing, 1874.

Arnot, David. *Animadversions on the Proceedings of the Regents of the Smithsonian Institution in their Choice of An Architect*. New York: Published for Circulation, 1847.

Baird, Donald. "Cloning a Dinosaur: Waterhouse Hawkins and the Skeleton of Hadrosaurus." Unpublished ms.

Beauchamp, Tanya Edwards. "Adolph Cluss: An Architect in Washington During the Civil War and Reconstruction." *Records of the Columbia Historical Society of Washington, D.C.* 1971–72, pp. 338–58.

Bell, Whitfield J. *A Cabinet of Curiosities: Five Episodes in the Evolution of American Museums*. Charlottesville: University Press of Virginia, 1967.

Bishop, Robert, and Patricia Coblentz. *The World of Antiques, Art, and Architecture in Victorian America*. New York: Dutton, 1979.

Bober, P. P., and R. O. Rubenstein. *Renaissance Artists and Antique Sculpture*. New York: Oxford University Press, 1987.

Bryan, John, ed. *Robert Mills*. Washington, D.C.: American Institute of Architects Press, 1989.

Cochrane, Rexmond C. *The National Academy of Sciences: Its First Hundred Years, 1863–1963*. Washington, D.C.: National Academy Press, 1978.

Cole, Donald B., and John J. McDonough, eds. *Benjamin Brown French: Witness to the Young Republic, A Yankee's Journal, 1828–1870*. Hanover, N.H.: University Press of New England, 1989.

Collins, Kathleen. *Washingtoniana Photographs: Collections in the Prints and Photographs Division of the Library of Congress*. Washington, D.C.: Superintendent of Documents, 1989.

Cook, Clarence. *The House Beautiful: Essays on Beds and Tables, Stools and Candlesticks*. New York: Scribners, 1881.

Downing, Andrew Jackson. *The Architecture of Country Houses*. D. Appleton, 1850. Reprint. New York: Dover, 1969.

Elliot, Clark A., comp. *Biographical Index to American Science: The Seventeenth Century to 1920*. Westport, Conn.: Greenwood Press, 1990.

Fleming, James Rodger. *Meteorology in America, 1800–1870*. Baltimore and London: Johns Hopkins University Press, 1990.

Gallagher, H. M. Pierce. *Robert Mills, Archi-*

tect of the Washington Monument, 1781–1855. New York: Columbia University Press, 1935.

Gillispie, Charles Coulston, ed. *Dictionary of Scientific Biography,* vol. 6. New York: Scribners, 1972.

Gilman, Roger. *Great Styles of Interior Architecture, With Their Decoration and Furniture.* New York: Harper, 1924.

Goode, George Brown. *The Smithsonian Institution, 1846–1896: The History of its First Half-Century.* Washington, D.C.: De Vinne Press, 1897.

Goode, James. *Capital Losses: A Cultural History of Washington's Destroyed Buildings.* Washington, D.C.: Smithsonian Institution Press, 1979.

———. *Outdoor Sculpture of Washington, D.C.* Washington, D.C.: Smithsonian Institution Press, 1974.

Greiff, Constance M. *John Notman, Architect.* Philadelphia: The Atheneum, 1979.

Grier, Katherine C. *Culture and Comfort: People, Parlors, and Upholstery, 1850–1930.* Rochester, N.Y.: Strong Museum, 1988.

Gutheim, Frederick. *The Federal City: Plans and Realities.* Washington, D.C.: Smithsonian Institution Press, 1976.

Hafertepe, Kenneth. *America's Castle: The Evolution of the Smithsonian Building and Its Institution, 1840–1878.* Washington, D.C.: Smithsonian Institution Press, 1984.

Hendrickson, Walter Brookfield. *David Dale Owen, Pioneer Geologist of the Middle West.* Indianapolis: Indiana Historical Bureau, 1943.

Hinsley, Curtis, Jr. *Savages and Scientists: The Smithsonian Institution and the Development of American Anthropology, 1846–1910.* Washington, D.C.: Smithsonian Institution Press, 1981.

Hunter, Alfred. *Washington and Georgetown Directory: Stranger's Guidebook and Congressional and Clerk's Register.* Washington, D.C.: Kirkwood & McGill, 1853.

Janson, H. W. *History of Art: A Survey of the Major Visual Arts from the Dawn of History to the Present Day.* New York: Abrams, 1973.

Jones, Owen. *The Grammar of Ornament.* London: Day & Son, 1856. Reprint. New York: Portland House, 1986.

Kohlstedt, Sally Gregory. "History in a Natural History Museum: George Brown Goode and the Smithsonian Institution." *The Public Historian,* vol. 10, no. 2 (Spring 1988), pp. 7–26.

Leopold, Richard. *Robert Dale Owen.* Cambridge, Mass.: Harvard University Press, 1940. Reprint. New York: Octagon Books, 1969.

Longstreth, Richard, ed. *The Mall in Washington, 1791–1991.* Studies in the History of Art, CASVA, Symposium Papers 14. Hanover, N.H., and London: National Gallery of Art Press, 1991.

Lowe, David. *Lost Chicago.* Boston: Houghton Mifflin, 1975.

McCutcheon, Mary. "The Children's Room at the Smithsonian: 1901 to 1939." *Curator,* vol. 35, no. 1 (March 1992), pp. 6–20.

Maury, William. *Alexander "Boss" Shepherd and the Board of Public Works.* George Washington University Washington Studies, no. 3. Washington, D.C., 1975.

Melnick, Marsha, and Susan E. Meyer, eds. *Nineteenth Century Furniture: Innovation, Revival and Reform.* New York: Billboard Publications, 1982.

Meyer, Franz S. *Meyer's Handbook of Ornament: The elements and application of decoration to all manner of interior and exterior architectural features, furnishing, utensils, jewelry, printing &c.* London: B. T. Batsford, 1894. Reprint. London: Omega Books, 1987.

Mills, Robert. *Papers of Robert Mills, 1781–1855.* Robert L. Alexander, ed. Wilmington, Del.: Scholarly Resources, 1990.

Molella, Arthur, Nathan Reingold, Marc Rothenberg, Joan Steiner, and Kathleen Waldenfels, *A Scientist in American Life: Essays and Lectures by Joseph Henry.* Washington, D.C.: Smithsonian Institution Press, 1980.

Montgomery, Florence M. *Textiles in America, 1650–1870: A Dictionary Based on Original Documents, Prints and Paintings, Commercial Records, American Merchants' Papers, Shopkeepers' Advertisements, and Pattern Books with Original Swatches of Cloth.* New York: Norton, 1984.

Moss, Roger W. *Lighting for Historic Buildings: A Guide to Selecting Reproductions.* Washington, D.C.: Preservation Press, 1988.

Myers, Denys Peter. *Gaslighting in America: A Guide for Historic Preservation.* Washington, D.C.: U.S. Department of the Interior, Office of Archeology and Historic Preservation, 1978.

Nabokov, Peter, and Robert Easton. *Native American Architecture.* New York: Oxford University Press, 1989.

NeCastro, Linda. "Grace Lincoln Temple and the Smithsonian's Children's Room of 1901." Unpublished master's thesis, Bryn Mawr College, 1988.

Newton, Roger Hale. *Town & Davis Architects: Pioneers in American Revivalist Architecture, 1812–1870.* New York: Columbia University Press, 1942.

Owen, Robert Dale. *Hints on Public Architecture.* Introduction by Cynthia R. Field. New York: Putnam, 1849. Reprint. New York: Da Capo Press, 1978.

———. *Threading My Way: An Autobiography.* New York: G. W. Carleton, 1874. Reprint. New York: Augustus M. Kelley, 1967.

Parker, John Henry. *A Glossary of Terms used in Grecian, Roman, Italian and Gothic Architecture.* 2d ed. London: Charles Tilt; Oxford: J. H. Parker, Leicester: T. Combe, 1838.

———. *A Handbook for Visitors to Oxford.* Oxford: John Henry Parker, 1847.

Parks, Edward, and Jean Paul Carlhian. *A New View from the Castle.* Washington, D.C.: Smithsonian Institution Press, 1987.

Peterson, Anne E. *Hornblower and Marshall, Architects.* Washington, D.C.: Preservation Press, 1978.

Poinsett, Joel R. *Discourse on the Objects and Importance of the National Institution for the Promotion of Science.* Washington, D.C.: P. Force, 1841.

Post, Robert. *The Centennial Exhibition: A Treatise upon Selected Aspects of the Great International Exhibition Held in Philadelphia on the Occasion of Our Nation's One Hundredth Birthday. . . .* Washington, D.C.: Smithsonian Institution Press, 1976.

Reingold, Nathan, ed. Arthur P. Molella and Stuart Pierson, asst. eds. *The Papers of Joseph Henry,* vol. 1. Washington, D.C.: Smithsonian Institution Press, 1972.

A Reprint of the Historic Mitchell, Vance & Co. Catalog, ca. 1876. Introduction by Denys Peter Myers. New York: Dover, 1984.

Rhees, William J. *An Account of the Smithsonian Institution, its Founder, Building, Operations, etc.* Washington, D.C.: Thomas McGill, 1857, 1859, 1865, 1869, 1880.

———. *Visitor's Guide to the Smithsonian Institution and the United States National Museum.* Washington, D.C.: Judd & Detweiler, 1880, 1881, 1883, 1884, 1885, 1886, 1889, 1891, 1892.

Rivinus, E. F., and E. M. Youssef. *Spencer Baird of the Smithsonian.* Washington, D.C., and London: Smithsonian Institution Press, 1992.

Rothenberg, Marc, ed. Kathleen W. Dorman,

John C. Rumm, and Paul H. Theerman, asst. eds. *The Papers of Joseph Henry,* vol. 6. Washington, D.C.: Smithsonian Institution Press, 1992.

Russell, Loris S. "Early Nineteenth-century Lighting." In Charles E. Peterson, ed., *Building Early America.* Radnor, Pa.: Chilton, 1976.

Ryder, Richard. "Dinosaurs Through the Stereoscope." *Stereo World,* March–April 1985, pp. 4–17, 39.

———. "Hawkins' Hadrosaurus: The Stereographic Record." *The Mosasaur* (Delaware Valley Paleontological Society), vol. 3 (1986), pp. 169–80.

———. "Megatherium: Stereo's Most Photographed Fossil." *Stereo World,* May–June 1984, pp. 20–25, 33.

Scott, Pamela, ed. *Guide and Index to the Papers of Robert Mills, 1781–1855.* Wilmington, Del.: Scholarly Resources, 1990.

Seale, William. *The Tasteful Interlude: American Interiors Through the Camera's Eye, 1860–1917.* Nashville, Tenn.: American Association for State and Local History, 1981.

Showalter, J. Camille, and Janice Driesbach, eds. *Wooton Patent Desks: A Place for Everything and Everything in Its Place.* Exhibition catalog published by the Indiana State Museum and the Oakland Museum, 1983.

Sloan, Samuel. *Homestead Architecture.* Philadelphia: Lippincott, 1867.

Sturtevant, William C., gen. ed., Wayne Suttles, vol. ed. *Handbook of North American Indians: Northwest Coast,* vol. 7. Washington, D.C.: Smithsonian Institution Press, 1990.

Thorton, Peter. *Authentic Decor: The Domestic Interior, 1620–1920.* New York: Viking, 1984.

U.S. Congress, Senate, Report of the Special Committee of the Board of Regents Rela-

tive to the Fire, 38th Congress, 2d session, February 21, 1865, S. Rept. 129.

Viola, Herman. *The Indian Legacy of Charles Bird King.* Washington, D.C.: Smithsonian Institution Press, 1976.

Viola, Herman, and Carolyn Margolis, eds. *Magnificent Voyagers: The Exploring Expedition, 1838–1842.* Washington, D.C.: Smithsonian Institution Press, 1985.

Von Rosenstiel, Helene, and Gail Caskey Winkler. *Floor Coverings for Historic Buildings.* Washington, D.C.: Preservation Press, 1988.

Walters, Betty Lawson. *The King of Desks: Wooten's Patent Secretary.* Washington, D.C.: Smithsonian Institution Press, 1969.

Wilk, Christopher. *Thonet: 150 Years of Furniture.* Woodbury, N.Y.: Barron's, 1981.

———. "Thonet and Bentwood," in *Nineteenth Century Furniture: Innovation, Revival and Reform.* Introduction by Mary Jean Madigan. Edited by Art & Antiques. New York: Billboard Publications, 1982.

Wilson, Richard Guy. *McKim, Mead & White, Architects.* New York: Rizzoli, 1983.

Withey, Henry F., and Elsie Rathburn Withey. *Biographical Dictionary of American Architects (Deceased).* Los Angeles: New Age, 1956.

Yochelson, Ellis. *National Museum of Natural History: 75 Years in the Natural History Building.* Washington, D.C.: Smithsonian Institution Press, 1985.

Index